fall 2022

Mission

The *Community Literacy Journal* is an interdisciplinary journal that publishes both scholarly work that contributes to theories, methodologies, and research agendas and work by literacy workers, practitioners, and community literacy program staff. We are especially committed to presenting work done in collaboration between academics and community members, organizers, activists, teachers, and artists.

We understand "community literacy" as including multiple domains for literacy work extending beyond mainstream educational and work institutions. It can be found in programs devoted to adult education, early childhood education, reading initiatives, or work with marginalized populations. It can also be found in more informal, ad hoc projects, including creative writing, graffiti art, protest songwriting, and social media campaigns.

For us, literacy is defined as the realm where attention is paid not just to content or to knowledge but to the symbolic means by which it is represented and used. Thus, literacy refers not just to letters and to text but to other multimodal, technological, and embodied representations, as well. Community literacy is interdisciplinary and intersectional in nature, drawing from rhetoric and composition, communication, literacy studies, English studies, gender studies, race and ethnic studies, environmental studies, critical theory, linguistics, cultural studies, education, and more.

Subscriptions

Donations to the *CLJ* in any amount can be made with a check made out to "FIU English Department," with *Community Literacy Journal* in the memo line.

Send to:

Paul Feigenbaum
Department of English
Florida International University
DM462D
11200 SW 8th St.
Miami, FL 33199

Donors at the $40 level or above will receive a courtesy print subscription of the academic year's issues.

Cover Artist and Art

Jen White-Johnson is an Afro-Latina disabled art activist, designer, and educator. Jen White-Johnson uses zines and collage art to explore the intersection of content and caregiving with an emphasis on redesigning ableist visual culture. Her creative practice shines best when she can infuse design justice, disability justice, photography, zine making, and art activism to center Afro-Latina and Neurodivergent creativity, care work, and joy as essential acts of resistance. *La Triguena Morena* is Jen's first collage portrait series that specifically centers Afro-Latina artists and designers whose creative practices are rooted in collective liberation, justice, equitable representation in art and design education, visual media, and disability culture. Despite the lack of consistent disability representation in Black and Brown communities, Jen believes that each of these creative forces should be honored and given their flowers now while they can still receive them. We must first connect with ourselves to connect with others. We develop an atmosphere for reflection and introspection and share our experiences and knowledge with others.

Jen has presented her activist work and collaborated with a number of brands and art spaces across print and digital such as Target, Converse, and Apple. Her photography and design work has been featured in The Washington Post, AfroPunk, Latina.com, and Teen Vogue and is permanently archived in libraries at The Metropolitan Museum of Art, and the National Museum of Women in the Arts. In 2021 she was listed as 20 Latino Artists to watch on Today.com. Jen currently teaches as Adjunct Faculty at the Maryland Institute College of Art, where she is also an alumnus, having received her MFA in Graphic Design in 2010. She currently lives in Baltimore with her husband and 10-year-old son.

Submissions

Submissions for the Articles section of the journal should clearly demonstrate engagement with community literacy scholarship, particularly scholarship previously published in the *Community Literacy Journal*. The editors seek work that pushes the field forward in exciting and perhaps unexpected ways. Case studies, qualitative and/or quantitative research, conceptual articles, etc., ranging from 25-30 manuscript pages, are welcome. If deemed appropriate, we will send the manuscript out to readers for blind review. You can expect a report in approximately 10-12 weeks.

Community Literacy Journal is committed to inclusive citation practices and encourages authors to cite and acknowledge ideas of BIPOC scholars, activists, and organizers in community literacy.

The *Community Literacy Journal* also welcomes shorter manuscripts (10-15 pages) for three sections reviewed in-house:

Community Literacy Project and Program Profiles will discuss innovative and impactful community-based projects and programs that are grounded in best practices. We encourage community-based practitioners and non-profit staff to submit for this section. Profiles should draw on community literacy scholarship, but they are not expected to have the extended lit reviews that are customary in the articles section of the journal. If you are a community member wanting to submit, and it is your first time writing for an academic journal, we are happy to offer mentorship and answer questions. Pieces co-authored by multiple stakeholders in a project are also welcome.

Please submit using our online submission system. Contact the Project and Program Profiles Editor, Vincent Portillo, with questions at portilvi@bc.edu.

Issues in Community Literacy will offer targeted analysis, reflection, and/or complication of ongoing challenges associated with the work of community literacy. Potential subjects for this section include (but are not limited to): building/sustaining infrastructure, navigating institutional constraints, pursuing community literacy in graduate school, working with vulnerable populations, building ethical relationships, realizing reciprocity, and negotiating conflicts among partners. We imagine this as a space for practitioners to raise critical issues or offer a response to an issue raised in a previous volume of the *CLJ*.

We encourage community-based practitioners and non-profit staff to submit for this section. If you are a community member wanting to submit, and it is your first time writing for an academic journal, we are happy to offer mentorship and answer questions. Pieces co-authored by multiple stakeholders in a project are also welcome.

Please submit using our online submission system. Contact the Issues in Community Literacy Editor, Cayce Wicks, with questions at cwick003@fiu.edu.

Coda: Community Writing and Creative Work welcomes submissions of poetry, creative nonfiction, short stories, and multigenre work on any topics that have ensued from community writing projects. This may be work about community writing projects, and this may be expressed in ways we have yet to imagine. We ask authors to include a personal reflection about the submission itself—information about your community writing group (if you belong to one); your personal journey as a writer; what inspired you to write your piece; and anything else you'd care to share about your life—as an invitation for the author and Coda's readers to consider writing and activism as intertwined.Contact Coda editors with questions at Coda.Editors@gmail.com.

Authors interested in reviewing for the CLJ should contact Book and New Media Review Editor Jessica Shumake at jessica.shumake@gmail.com.

Advertising

Community Literacy Journal welcomes advertising. The journal is published twice annually, in the Fall and Spring (November and May). Deadlines for advertising are two months prior to publication (September and March).

Ad Sizes and Pricing

Half page (trim size 5.5 x 4.25): $200
Full page (trim size 5.5 x 8.5): $350
Inside back cover (trim size 5.5 x 8.5): $500
Inside front cover (trim size 5.5 x 8.5): $600

Format

We accept .PDF, .JPG, .TIF or .EPS. All advertising images should be camera-ready and have a resolution of 300 dpi. For more information, please contact Veronica House (housev@colorado.edu) and Paul Feigenbaum (pfeigenb@fiu.edu).

Copyright © 2022 *Community Literacy Journal*
ISSN 1555-9734

Community Literacy Journal is a member of the Council of Editors of Learned Journals.

Production and distribution managed by Parlor Press.

community literacy journal

Publication of the *Community Literacy Journal* is made possible through the generous support of the English Department and the Writing and Rhetoric Program at Florida International University. The *CLJ* is a journal of the Coalition for Community Writing. Current issues and archives are available open access at https://digitalcommons.fiu.edu/communityliteracy/

Editorial Board

Jonathan Alexander, *University of California Irvine*
Steven Alvarez, *St. John's University*
April Baker Bell, *Michigan State University*
Kirk Branch, *Montana State University*
Laurie Cella, *Shippensburg University*
David Coogan, *Virginia Commonwealth University*
Ellen Cushman, *Northeastern University*
Lisa Dush, *DePaul University*
Jenn Fishman, *Marquette University*
Linda Flower, *Carnegie Mellon University*
Laurie Grobman, *Pennsylvania State University Berks*
Shirley Brice Heath, *Stanford University*
Glenn Hutchinson, *Florida International University*
Tobi Jacobi, *Colorado State University*
Ben Kuebrich, *West Chester University*
Carmen Kynard, *Texas Christian University*
Paula Mathieu, *Boston College*
Seán Ronan McCarthy, *James Madison University*
Michael Moore, *DePaul University*
Beverly Moss, *The Ohio State University*
Steve Parks, *The University of Virginia*
Jessica Pauszek, *Boston College*
Eric Darnell Pritchard, *University of Arkansas Fayetteville*
Jessica Restaino, *Montclair State University*
Elaine Richardson, *The Ohio State University*
Lauren Rosenberg, *University of Texas at El Paso*
Tiffany Rousculp, *Salt Lake Community College*
Iris Ruiz, *University of California Merced*
Donnie Sackey, *University of Texas at Austin*
Rachael W. Shah, *University of Nebraska-Lincoln*
Erec Smith, *York College of Pennsylvania*
Stephanie Wade, *Stony Brook University*
Christopher Wilkey, *Northern Kentucky University*

fall 2022

COMMUNITY LITERACY Journal

Editors	Paul Feigenbaum, *Florida International University*
	Veronica House, *University of Denver*
Senior Assistant Editor and Issues in Community Literacy Editor	Cayce Wicks, *Florida International University*
Journal Manager	Erin Daugherty, *University of Arkansas at Fayetteville*
Book and New Media Review Editor	Jessica Shumake, *University of Notre Dame*
Consulting Editor and Project Profiles Editor	Vincent Portillo, *Boston College*
Coda: Community Writing and Creative Work Editorial Collective	Kefaya Diab, *University of North Carolina at Charlotte*
	Leah Falk, *Rutgers University, Camden*
	Chad Seader, *William Penn University*
	Alison Turner, *ACLS Leading Edge Fellow, Jackson, Mississippi*
	Stephanie Wade, *Stony Brook University*
Senior Copyeditor	Elvira Carrizal-Dukes, *University of Texas at El Paso*
Copyeditors	Charisse Iglesias, *Community-Campus Partnerships for Health*
	Walter Lucken IV, *Wayne State University*
	Christine Martorana, *Florida International University*
	Keshia Mcclantoc, *University of Nebraska-Lincoln*

COMMUNITY LITERACY Journal

Fall 2022
Volume 17, Issue 1

1   *Guest Editors' Introduction*
      Ada Hubrig and Christina V. Cedillo

Articles

8   *Documenting Barriers, Transforming Academic Cultures: A Study of the Critical Access Literacies of the CCCC Accessibility Guides*
      Ruth Osorio

25 *Storying Access: Citizen Journalism, Disability Justice, and the Kansas City Homeless Union*
      Brynn Fitzsimmons

40 *Everything You Need to Eat: Food, Access, and Community*
      Tyler Martinez

49 *Rethinking Access: Recognizing Privileges and Positionalities in Building Community Literacy*
      Sweta Baniya

65 *Reinventing a Cultural Practice of Interdependence to Counter the Transnational Impacts of Disabling Discourses*
      Elenore Long

Symposium

93 *To Community with Care: Enacting Positive Barriers to Access as Good Relations*
      Cana Uluak Itchuaqiyaq, Caroline Gottschalk Druschke, Lauren Cagle, and Rachel Bloom-Pojar

96 *No, I won't introduce you to my mama: Boundary Spanners, Access, and Accountability to Indigenous Communities*
Cana Uluak Itchuaqiyaq

99 *Cultivating Soil, Cultivating Self*
Lauren E. Cagle

103 *Co-Creating Stories of Confianza*
Rachel Bloom-Pojar

107 *From Access to Refusal: Remaking University-Community Collaboration*
Caroline Gottschalk Druschke

Book and New Media Reviews

116 *From the Book and New Media Review Editor's Desk*
Jessica Shumake

117 *Rhetoric Inc: Ford's Filmmaking and the Rise of Corporatism* by Timothy Johnson
Reviewed by Geoffrey Clegg

122 *Women's Ways of Making,* edited by Maureen Daly Goggin and Shirley K Rose
Reviewed by Kristen A. Ruccio

129 *Writing for Love and Money: How Migration Drives Literacy Learning in Transnational Families* by Kate Vieira
Reviewed by Jagadish Paudel

fall 2022

Guest Editors' Introduction

Access as Community Literacy: A Call for Intersectionality, Reciprocity, and Collective Responsibility

Ada Hubrig and Christina V. Cedillo

Abstract

> In this guest editors' introduction to *Community Literacy Journal's* special issue on access, the guest editors call for greater attention to access work *as* community literacy, pushing for the field to tend to issues of intersectionality, reciprocity, and collective access in community literacy work. This introduction previews the work of the special issue's contributors and puts their work in conversation with ongoing work in critical disability studies, disability activism, and disability justice.

Keywords

> access, disability, disability justice, labor

Our embodied experiences as multiply marginalized disabled people have left us apprehensive about matters of access: Systemic inequalities often render access a seeming bonus measure that one must fight for at great personal cost. The sheer amount of physical and emotional labor involved in securing accommodations or even some measure of consideration means that many vulnerable people go without the care or resources they need, worn out by the constant struggle (see Konrad's concept of "Access Fatigue"). These inequalities are often reproduced in community literacy contexts, especially when overshadowed by university and college agendas (see Kannan et. al). Currently, we bear witness as institutions within (and outside of) academia proclaim the arrival of "post-COVID" times and rush a return to "normal." Their performative inspirational gestures attempt to hide the privileging of profit and protocol over human safety, but they don't do so very well.

This deliberate erasure of harmful conditions proves nothing new to members of marginalized communities, against whose bodyminds normalcy is established. We know that long before the arrival of the pandemic, many people's physical and mental wellbeing were threatened by the existing inequities associated with the normal that these institutions want so urgently to re-establish. For those of us who are marginalized, COVID intensified how the lack of access and support accelerates the physical dangers always already present in our lives. For many others, previously unaccustomed to having to constantly negotiate for their own access needs, the pandemic lay bare the failure of institutions to address real human needs.

However, the pandemic also exposed (we hope) how systemic inequities work by isolating targeted persons, framing the struggle for access as an individual exhausting process rather than a process that should bring people together to enact change. Hence, "Access is Love," write disability activists Mia Mingus, Alice Wong, and Sandy Ho, ". . . a collective responsibility instead of a sole responsibility placed on a few individuals" (DVP). Like Mingus, Wong, and Ho, we believe that love entails appreciating one another's diverse needs and the different forms of access that they necessitate while still prioritizing those most in need. Love means practicing a communal solidarity across difference that does not erase people's complex and relative positionalities as we work side by side. As disability rhetorics teacher/researchers, we (Ada and Christina) argue that this goal demands our recognition of access as an issue that informs but transcends disability. Without ignoring or erasing the many important and ongoing critical conversations among disability activists and scholars, what we mean is, ensuring access is EVERYONE's responsibility, not just the charge of disabled people who are frequently tired and burnt out from working toward access on our own.

In response to the institutional push to put the labor of access on individuals, in this issue we focus on *access* as a concept that centers intersectionality, collective responsibility, and community to challenge oppressive logics. As Ada has argued, this kind of mutual "reciprocity rejects models of university community-engagement that suggests the university as a benevolent, morally superior institution serving the community and bestowing its intellectual gift" ("We Move Together" 149). Here, we hold space for critical conversations that aim to decenter traditional loci of power, those institutions that simultaneously cause harm and claim authority to rectify said harm, to intentionally highlight the power and potential of community-based access work.

Access as Political, Access as the Start

As the work of disability justice collectives like Sins Invalid illustrates, access isn't neutral, and politics of access are fraught with oppressive power dynamics that reflect the political agendas of the institutions that offer access to some and deny it to others. As designer, researcher, and disability justice organizer Aimi Hamraie has argued through their critical history of the Universal Design Movement, who experiences access (and barriers to access) is a product of mutually enacted epistemology, politics, and how these are applied to the built environment (18). In other words, access reflects the politics, values, and ways of knowing held by the institutions granting and foreclosing access. Because their dominant frameworks for deciphering people's access needs typically center privileged bodyminds, these institutions can then ignore the needs of multiply marginalized people while claiming that they are doing the work. Furthermore, they orient public attention towards certain expressions of need and access work, and away from others in social, cultural, and material ways, meaning that people's needs are ignored if they do not align with mainstream impressions of what that looks like (see Schalk 6, Pickens 95).

For those doing community literacy work adjacent to university or collegiate power structures, access—and lack of access—frequently replicate the same white supremacist, cisheteropatriarchal, ableist normativities of institutions: access is granted unevenly around race, ethnicity, gender, sexuality, nationality, social class, disability, and other positionalities. Questions of access lay these power dynamics bare: who has access to community literacy? Who has access to university credentialing and resources and why? How do universities demand access to marginalized communities while denying access to people from those same communities? How do community literacy programs create access for marginalized people?

At the same time, we understand access is not the end goal. We echo late disability justice activist Stacey Milbern, "But Access is only the first step in movement building. People talk about access as the outcome, not the process, as if having spaces be accessible is enough to get us all free" (qtd. in Piepzna-Samarasinha, 129). While we understand access has material consequences for many people, we also understand that granting access on an individualized basis itself is not a panacea to rectify the deeply ingrained inequalities and interlocking systems of oppression that blocked access in the first place. Lack of access is a systemic problem linked to the logics of colonialism, capitalism, and white supremacy. As Piepzna-Samarsinha argues, the dismissal of the needs and lives of disabled—and especially multiply marginalized disabled people—is the direct result of colonization and enslavement that violently categorized many bodies as undeserving of access and care and dignity (130).

Compounding these problems is the issue of labor and how access work is disproportionately assigned to and expected of marginalized people. Already fatigued individuals are expected to not only advocate for themselves but for others, too often without the physical and financial support granted to debilitating institutions themselves. Even when we take on that labor willingly and lovingly, it can still be taxing. In "On 'Crip Doulas,' Invisible Labor, and Surviving Academia while Disabled," Ada addresses this problem in relation to disability and disabled care work. They write, "While I enjoy doing this work, it is *work*." Such care work can include helping others as they come to claim their disability, begin to navigate the altogether complex processes of seeking accommodations, and struggle against the sociopolitical and material erasure of disability and disabled people. It also means being mindful regarding how much labor we expect from others and ourselves. However, as Ada also notes, "Attending to these dynamics is central to interrogating how—even within disability spaces—white supremacist, heteropatriarchal crap still gets centered." As Christina, Ersula J. Ore, and Kimberly Gail Wieser argue in "Diversity is not an End Game: BIPOC Futures in the Academy," even supposed safe spaces can re-/traumatize those targeted by racism. Therefore, doing the work of access necessarily requires that we attend to "the myriad ways that BIPOC are [already] forced to experience duress, navigate threatening spaces, and leverage precious resources" in order to survive. Engaging race without disability or disability without race proves harmful to the lives and interests of multiply marginalized people and reinscribes the social centrality of privileged bodyminds. Thus, unless we engage access intersectionality, our attempts to build communities of care can still lead to demands for extra labor from those who are most vulnerable. If so, they replicate the very oppressions that target multiply marginalized people primarily but ultimately harm us all.

Accessibility should be centered in the creation and maintaining of intersectional and interdependent praxes with careful attention to *who* is being asked to shoulder the labor of access, or else we actively practice exclusion. We believe that centering accessibility as an intersectional issue will extend ongoing conversations in community literacy studies, such as conversations around labor, ethics, and reciprocity (Miller et. al.; Shah), around the centering of whiteness and white supremacy (Garcia; Jackson and Whitehorse DeLaune; Kynard), and what Carmen Kynard has referred to as *"the work"* of community literacy studies. Although the word "accessibility" is closely associated with disability, our special issue of *Community Literacy Journal* seeks to examine the interactive forces that enable or preclude access.

Access in Community Literacy Studies

Access isn't the end goal, but it is an important start. As disabled oracle Alice Wong argues, "We all have the capacity to create access for one another. And while things still feel bleak, I have hope for the future, because we all have the potential to learn and grow if we close the distance together" (306). Wong asks us to think more critically about who are excluded from the spaces we inhabit and what we can do to create access for those excluded. In this special issue of *Community Literacy Journal*, we center work on access, collectively imagining how community literacy practitioners might "close the distance" and center accessibility, as well as offer critical insight into the tensions inherent in access work.

In the first article in this special issue, Ruth Osorio offers a vision of critical access literacies. In "Documenting Barriers, Transforming Academic Cultures: A Study of the Critical Access Literacies of the CCCC Accessibility Guides," Osorio traces the history of the Conference on College Composition and Communication (CCCCs) Accessibility Guides, centering the labor and wisdom of multiply-marginalized disabled scholars. Osorio highlights "how critical access literacies can be practiced to dismantle ableist structures while building a world for disability liberation," a project that takes up anti-ableist praxis to reimagine institutions—and hold them accountable.

Offering insight into another form of access in community literacy work, Brynn Fitzsimmons takes up media coverage of the Kansas City Homeless Union through decarceral and disability justice frameworks. In "Storying Access: Citizen Journalism, Disability Justice, and the KC Homeless Union," they task community literacy practitioners with more thoughtfully engaging intersectionality and interrogating how community literacy practitioners are still "practicing complicity with white supremacist, settler colonial, carceral logics," examining how the way stories are told about homelessness can create pathways or blocks to access.

Tyler Martinez expands notions of access in food literacy. In Martinez's "Everything You Need to Eat: Food, Access, and Community," Martinez calls for more thorough exploration of food access, and the roles and ethical obligations communities and institutions in sponsoring food literacy, critiquing the "disciplinary colorblindness" asking for a more intersectional, interdisciplinary approach to food literacy.

Taking up digital literacy access, Sweta Baniya offers her insights into access through her community literacy efforts in Nepal. "Rethinking Access: Recognizing Privileges and Positionalities in building community literacy," Sweta Baniya engages access—and barriers to access—through her involvement with Nepalese community literacy programs. Baniya focuses on access to digital literacy and its many ramifications for the lived experiences of the Nepalese people, reminding us, "Digital literacy and access are a collective responsibility."

In "Reinventing a Cultural Practice of Interdependence to Counter the Transnational Impacts of Disabling Discourses," Elenore Long traces how a group of Nuer, Dinka, and Arab women theorize thanduk as a community literacy practice, and how thanduk functions as an anticolonialist practice that enables access: "In thanduk, they are each theorizing this individual experience with people who are experiencing different individual experiences navigating the same systems." In taking up thanduk as a community literacy practice alongside the women engaging in these practices, Long asks us to consider how access has been limited and curtailed and to ask, "how could things be otherwise?"

Concluding the articles of the special issue on access is a symposium that inverts the question of access, critically examining the tensions that arise when it's institutions seeking access. Their work reminds us that sometimes barriers are important and necessary, especially when we are considering how institutions demand access to marginalized communities. In the symposium, "To Community with Care: Enacting Positive Barriers to Access as Good Relations," symposium contributors offer insights across positionalities to center the needs of communities and relationships and argue for the importance of maintaining barriers even as institutions demand access to these communities—often in exploitative ways.

In each section of this symposium, authors expand on the ethics of access between marginalized communities and institutional demands/expectations. Cana Uluak Itchuaqiyaq, in their symposium section "No, I won't introduce you to my mama: Boundary spanners, access, and accountability to Indigenous communities," Itchuaqiyaq offers insight into institutional demands for access to her Iñupiat community: "Let's unpack what asking me to make introductions in my community means. What I'm really being asked to do is use my personal relationships that I've spent a lifetime building and rebuilding for their academic research needs. [. . .] That's some bullshit," pushing academics to be more accountable to communities as the central focus of community engaged work. In "Cultivating Soil, Cultivating Self," Lauren E. Cagle pushes us to think about how—as a university professor—is a defacto gatekeeper to institutional resources: "I am often in a position to offer academia's resources to those I am in relation with, including those academia may not have invited in," asking community literacy practitioners with institutional ties to more ethically consider how we leverage those resources. In Rachel Bloom-Pojar's "Co-creating stories of confianza," Bloom-Pojar interrogates how white academics often objectify Latinx communities and commodify Latinx stories, offering through her own community literacy experiences thoughts on access and ethics. In "From Access to Refusal: Remaking University-Community Collaboration," Caroline Gottschalk Druschke shares insight into her experiences in community literacy work, offering a framework for "remaking university-community collaboration in ways that support good relations– relations that support community-driven efforts, relations that refuse the expectations of the university, relations that nourish those involved–and make space inside of and despite exploitative university structures for collaboration and refusal." Taken together, the Symposium challenges community literacy practitioners with institutional ties to more critically examine our complicity in exploitative, patriarchal, and white supremacist institutional practices.

Coda: Creating Collective Access, Fostering Community

Disability justice recognizes that "to live and create change, we must work in connection both with ourselves and with one another" (Kafai 173). We reject the institutional models that grant access to the privileged and withhold it from the marginalized—recognizing these are the very processes and systems by which privileges and marginalizations are created in the first place (Cedillo "What Does it Mean"; Hubrig "Liberation"). We are grateful to the contributors of this special issue who ask us to more deeply consider issues of access in community literacy work, as well as *Community Literacy Journal* editors Veronica House and Paul Feigenbaum and their editorial team for inviting us to center issues of access in this special issue. Learning from the work of disability justice organizers, we know that community, while imperfect, is the only way forward.

Works Cited / Consulted

Cedillo, Christina V. "Disabled and Undocumented: In/Visibility at the Borders of Presence, Disclosure, and Nation." *Rhetoric Society Quarterly*, vol. 50, no. 3, 2020, pp. 203-211.

—. "What Does It Mean to Move? Race, Disability, and Critical Embodiment Pedagogy." *Composition Forum*, vol. 39, 2018, (np). https://www.compositionforum.com/issue/39/to-move.php.

Cedillo, Christina V., Ersula J. Ore, and Kimberly Gail Wieser. "Diversity is not an End Game: BIPOC Futures in the Academy." *Present Tense: A Journal of Rhetoric in Society*, vol. 9, no. 2, 2022.

Disability Visibility Project [DVP]. "Access is Love." *Disability Visibility Project*. 2019.

Hamraie, Aimi. *Building Access: Universal Design and the Politics of Disability*. U of Minnesota P, 2017.

Hubrig, Ada. "'Liberation Happens When We All Get Free'—or—Disability Justice Academia Isn't." *Spark: A 4C4Equality Journal*, vol. 4, 2022.

—"On 'Crip Doulas,' Invisible Labor, and Surviving Academia While Disabled." *The Journal of Multimodal Rhetorics*, vol. 5, no. 1, 2021.

—. "'We Move Together': Reckoning with Disability Justice in Community Literacy Studies." *Community Literacy Journal*, vol. 14, no. 2, 2020, pp. 144-153.

Hubrig, Ada, and Ruth Osorio (Editors). "Symposium: Enacting a Culture of Access in Our Conference Spaces." *College Composition and Communication*, vol. 72, no. 1, 2020, pp. 87-117.

Jackson, Rachel C., and Dorothy Whitehorse DeLaune. "Decolonizing Community Writing with Community Listening: Story, Transrhetorical Resistance, and Indigenous Cultural Literacy Activism." *Community Literacy Journal*, vol. 13, no. 1, 2018, pp. 37-54.

Kafai, Shadya. *Crip Kinship: The Disability Justice & Art Activism of Sins Invalid*. Arsenal Pulp P, 2021.

Kannan, Vani, Ben Kuebrich, and Yanira Rodríguez. "Unmasking Corporate-Military Infrastructure: Four Theses." *Community Literacy Journal*, vol. 11, no. 1, 2016, pp. 76-93.

Konrad, Annika M. "Access Fatigue: The Rhetorical Work of Disability in Everyday Life." *College English*, vol. 83, no. 3, 2021, pp. 179-199.

Kynard, Carmen. "'All I Need is One Mic': A Black Feminist Community Meditation on the Work, the Job, and the Hustle (and Why So Many of Yall Confuse This Stuff)." Conference on Community Writing, 18 Oct. 2019, Irvine Auditorium, University of Pennsylvania. Keynote Address.

Miller, Elizabeth, Anne Wheeler, and Stephanie White. "Keywords: Reciprocity." *Community Literacy Journal*, vol. 5, no. 2, 2011, pp. 171-178.

Pickens, Therí A. "Blue Blackness, Black Blueness: Making Sense of Blackness and Disability." *African American Review*, vol. 50, no. 2, 2017, pp. 93-103.

Piepzna-Samarasinha, Leah Lakshmi. *Care Work: Dreaming Disability Justice*. Arsenal Pulp Press. 2018.

—. "To Survive the Trumpocalypse, We Need Wild Disability Justice Dreams." *Truthout*. 2018.

Schalk, Sami. *Black Disability Politics*. Duke University Press, 2022.

Shah, Rachael W. *Rewriting Partnerships: Community Perspectives on Community-Based Learning*. Utah State University Press, 2020.

Skin, Tooth, and Bone: The Basis of Movement is Our People. Sins Invalid. 2nd ed., digital ed., 2019.

Wong, Alice. *Year of the Tiger: An Activist's Life*. Vintage Books. 2022.

Author Bios

Ada Hubrig (they/them; Twitter @AdamHubrig) is an autistic, nonbinary, multiply-disabled caretaker of cats. They live in Huntsville, Texas, where they work as an assistant professor and co-Writing Program Administrator for the English Department at Sam Houston State University as their day job. Their research centers disability, gender, and queerness and is featured in *College Composition and Communication*, *Reflections*, and *Composition Studies* among other places, and their words have also found homes in *Brevity* and *Disability Visibility Blog*. Ada is currently managing editor of the *Journal of Multimodal Rhetorics* and editor of the new *Journal of Disability in Writing, Rhetoric, and Literacy Studies*.

Christina V. Cedillo (she/they) is an associate professor of writing and rhetoric at the University of Houston-Clear Lake. Their research draws from cultural rhetorics and decolonial theory to focus on embodied rhetorics and rhetorics of embodiment at the intersections of race, gender, and disability, particularly in relation to Latinx rhetorics and critical pedagogies.

Articles

Documenting Barriers, Transforming Academic Cultures: A Study of the Critical Access Literacies of the CCCC Accessibility Guides

Ruth Osorio

Abstract

This article situates the practice of composing CCCC Accessibility Guides in critical access studies (Hamraie) and introduces the concept of critical access literacies. I argue that CCCC access guides cultivate critical access literacies amongst the guide writers and disabled and nondisabled conference participants, empowering them to better observe access barriers and advocate for expansive access. To make this argument, I triangulate interviews I conducted with the authors of the first six years of the guides (2011-2016) with textual analysis of the guides themselves. The interviews illustrate how the guide's early authors re-imagined access to include expansive and intersectional access needs.

Keywords

access, critical access literacies, CCCC Accessibility Guides, disability, conference access

Each year, as the Conference of College Composition and Communication (CCCC) attendees prepare for our trip to the annual conference, we engage with several different genres, including the call for papers, the program, registration portal, hotel registration, standing group announcements on WPA-L, and more.[1] Starting in 2011, a new genre entered the conference scene: the CCCC Accessibility Guide. Initiated and written by disability rhetoric scholar Margaret Price, the three-page single-spaced document and accompanying Flickr photo album documented the access barriers and affordances of traveling to Atlanta and the conference venue and hotels. Price described the elevators in Atlanta airport, identified restaurants with gluten-free options, and photographed the hallways and bathrooms at the Marriott Marquis. The Accessibility Guide was celebrated not only by disabled CCCC members but also by the institution itself; program chair Malea Powell thanked Price "for her generous work in providing accessibility information and feedback to make the convention as accessible as possible for all participants" in her greeting in the CCCC 2011 program (6).

What was started by Price in 2011 is now a standard genre for conference organizers in the profession. Every year since 2011, the Committee on Disability Issues in College Composition (CDICC) identifies volunteers to write the guide and supports them through the process. The volunteers then perform an accessibility audit of conference spaces, documenting and assessing the different features – entrances, hallways, bathroom stall widths – in terms of accessibility. After the volunteers write up their findings, revise, and then finalize the guide, the staff at NCTE/CCCC post it on the CCCC homepage, promote it on social media, and share it in emails to conference attendees. Just as the guide's reach has expanded, so has the guide itself. Price's guide contained three pages of single-spaced written content and an online photo album. The 2019 CCCC Accessibility Guide,[2] for the last in-person CCCC meeting since the onset of COVID-19, featured 80 pages of written and visual content. The expanded guide features information on local pharmacies, the lactation room, carpet patterns, shuttle information, and pool access options at the conference hotels.

The guides have become both a source of pride and source of frustration for the volunteer guide writers. By anticipating potential access needs of conference attendees, the writers of the accessibility guides make known the presence of disabled, sick, and Othered bodies in the profession. The guides have become part of the genre system of the CCCC convention, a genre devoted to making visible what is so often hidden in academic spaces: that we scholar-teachers do indeed have embodied needs, and thus, experience frailty to varying extents. And yet, for some of the guide writers, the guides also represent the organization's eagerness to delegate access labor to volunteers rather than centralize that work into the organization's *ethos* and practices. In other words, why is the responsibility of making known the presence of disabled, sick, and Othered bodies in the profession the responsibility of a small group of volunteers? The Access Guides provide a case study of not only disability justice in community literacy contexts but also the tension between grassroots disability activism and organizational rhetoric.

At first glance, the guides might appear to be more informative, technical documents than radical manifestos. However, after analyzing the guides and speaking with the authors, I believe that CCCC Accessibility Guides cultivate critical access literacies amongst guide writers, disabled CCCC members, and nondisabled conference participants. By approaching access as a collective responsibility, the guide empowers its creators and interpreters to better observe access barriers and advocate for expansive access. Critical access literacies are informed by the principles of Disability Justice (DJ), which in the words of Leah Lakshmi Piepzna-Samarasinha, asks the question:

> What does it mean to shift our idea of access and care (whether it's disability, childcare, economic access, or many more) from an individual chore, an unfortunate cost of having an unfortunate body, to a collective responsibility that's maybe even joyful? (33)

Piepzna-Samarasinha envisions disability as something to embrace rather than something to fix, and thus, approaches access as a collective responsibility rather than an individual burden. Critical access literacies, then, are interactive processes of composing, circulating, and responding to texts that create spaces of belonging for disabled people. They do so by merging DJ principles with the practices of community literacy, the "literate action[s] taken to support agency, understanding, and justice; and a rhetorical act built on the social ethic; and a strategic practice of intercultural inquiry" (Flowers 7). Critical access literacies, thus, are literate practices that invite both the composers and the readers across disabled identities to critique manifestations of ableism and foster an intersectional, collective culture of access.

In this article, I argue that the CCCC Accessibility Guides demonstrate how critical access literacies can spark knowledge-making about accessibility in organizational contexts. By introducing the concept of critical access literacies, I aim to show how the processes of writing and circulating guides build knowledge about access as a collective responsibility and intersectional access within the writing studies profession. These claims emerge from a study I conducted of the first six years of the CCCC accessibility guides (2011-2016), triangulating close reading of the guides themselves and interviews with the early guides' authors. In the summer of 2017, I interviewed Margaret Price (2011 Author, Atlanta), Muffy Walter (2012 Author, St. Louis), Tracy Donhardt (2014 Author, Indianapolis), Lauren Cagle (2015 Co-Author, Tampa), Ellie Browning (2015 Co-Author, Tampa), Casie Cobos (2016 Co-Author, Houston),[3] and Jay Dolmage (CDICC Chair from 2011-2015 and uncredited author of the 2013 guide) over Skype or phone, depending on the preference of the author.[4] While the guides themselves illustrate the possibilities of critical access literacies in the profession, the interviews showcase the literate practices that weave together disabled wisdom, intersectional awareness, and collaborative meaning-making. In the next section, I define what I call critical access literacies, literate practices that critique depoliticized ideologies of access and disability. Then, I analyze how the guide authors practiced critical access literacies informed by disability justice principles, focusing on collective access and intersectionality. In this analysis, I foreground not only the transformative possibility of the guides but also their limitations, particularly when institutions do not prioritize access in their decision-making processes.

Defining Critical Access Literacies

I will start with what critical access literacies are *not*: they are not bound by legalistic understandings of disability and liability. Critical access literacies counters mainstream access communication, in which access is typically defined in terms of accommodations granted to an individual by an institution. See, for instance, the disability policy for faculty at an urban, public university in the Mid-Atlantic, "Mid-Atlantic University will provide reasonable accommodation to a qualified individual with a disability in order to enable such individual to perform the essential functions of position for which he or she is applying or in which he or she is employed." Much of this language comes directly from federal legislation that aims to quantify disability, reasonableness, and accommodations. Such federal legislation has been hard-fought by disabled activists and has opened opportunities for disabled people, especially in educational and employment settings. However, a legalistic approach to access values productivity over humanity, individualism over community, and inclusion over justice. It manifests in what Jay Dolmage calls retrofitting: "to retrofit is to add a component or accessory to something that has already been manufactured or built. This retrofit does not necessarily make the product function, does not necessarily fix a faulty product, but it acts as a sort of correction" ("Mapping" 20). But it's not disabled people who need to be fixed, as Dolmage argues, but rather the environment and culture that excludes them. In contrast to retrofitting, critical access literacies are the interactive meaning-making activities that foster anti-ableist critique of the barriers disabled people face and empower community members to create disability-affirming spaces. I aim to situate critical access literacies in critical access studies, an emerging field named by Aimi Hamraie that critiques dominant, white-centered and depoliticized models of access. Situating this practice within Disability Justice and community literacies, I define each word in the phrase *critical access literacies* in the following paragraphs.

The *critical* in critical access literacies emphasizes the need to go beyond merely communicating the process of gaining accommodations in a specific setting: to be critical requires analyzing and critiquing ableist structures in society. As Hamraie explains, critical conveys both urgency – robust access *is* important – and the need for critique ("Making Access Critical"). Any sort of critical literacy "has an explicit aim of the critique and transformation of dominant ideologies, cultures and economies, and institutions and political systems" (Luke 5). By practicing critical access literacies, creators and interpreters[5] develop a more astute awareness of how ableist ideologies, systems, and design impede relationship-building for disabled people. But critical doesn't just imply destruction; critical also invites imagination, a core practice of Disability Justice. Shayda Kafai describes the vitality of imagining in DJ work: "creating new realities requires imagination. It requires rousing inventiveness. Dreaming a reality that holds space for all our intersectional bodyminds is how we declare ourselves in a world that, as Audre Lorde writes, 'we were never meant to survive'" (35). Being critical invites us to question the unquestioned, to see in between and beyond what is presented to us and imagine a new world. Critical access literacies cultivate disability consciousness by inviting creators and readers to deepen their understanding of disability as an embodied, political, and relational experience.

In a critical access literacy framework, *access* is envisioned as an act of love, a concept authored by disability justice activists Mia Mingus, Alice Wong, and Sandy Ho. Mingus expands in a solo-authored keynote speech, "Access for the sake of access or inclusion is not necessarily liberatory, but access done in the service of love, justice, connection and community is liberatory and has the power to transform" ("Disability Justice"). What Mingus, Wong, and Ho identify are the affective, relational dynamics of access. Within this framework, access isn't just being permitted entrance into a space, but rather, access is a sense of belonging in the space. And disabled people need more than just ramps to feel cared for and loved; they need a recognition of their mindbody's various needs and enthusiasm from the community to meet those needs. To create a sense of belonging, too, requires an acknowledgment that disabled people also occupy different embodied identities, and thus an intersectional approach is necessary. Just as Hamraie's conception of critical access studies "centers intersections of disability with race, gender, class, and aging" in its study of access across space and time, critical access literacies also demand an intersectional approach (*Building Access* 14). Pulling together the affective, relational, and intersectional threads, a critical access literacies framework defines access as the dynamic, collective work of creating spaces where multiply-marginalized disabled people with a wide range of needs can engage, connect, create, and lead now and if they want.

Critical access literacies are the literate activities that bring this vision of access to life. As community literacy scholars have long argued, *literacy* encompasses so much more than the act of learning to read and write in a classroom setting. Indeed, the field is invested in studying the "constellation of people, practices, and institutions that inform how people work with (and are worked by) texts" (Sheridan-Rabideau 3). Literacy happens in activist settings, as change-makers develop meaning-making practices that foster survival (Richardson), identity-formation (Darnell Pritchard), and activist consciousness (Flannery) in an oppressive world. Like Elenore Long, I'm interested in behind-the-scenes work that enables ordinary people to intervene in public discourse, the "literacies [that] organize how people carry out their purposes for going public" (16). When marginalized groups are not granted platforms in the public sphere, they create their own literate practices to bring their knowledge, critiques, and visions for the future to the public. Long's emphasis on going public is key to this study; critical access literacies blur the lines between public and private, fostering individual and community consciousness in small group settings while also agitating against ableist institutions, ideologies, and cultures. Within CCCC, disability activists developed critical access literacies to address access barriers, educate the nondisabled membership about disability and access, and ultimately forward a more intersectional, radical notion of access within a professional organization.

The Critical Access Literacies of the CCCC Guides

Academia has not historically been kind or welcoming to disabled scholars, and conferences are no exception. As argued by Margaret Price, Jay Dolmage, Tanya Titchkosky, M. Remi Yergeau, and so many others, academia professes allegiance to rationality, mental fitness, and productivity – qualities that define able-bodiedness and able-mindedness. Titchkosky argues in *The Question of Access*, "within the everyday practices and procedures of university environments… disability [is seen as] a problem in need of a solution" (70). Academia's resistance to making space for disability is especially apparent at conferences. Margaret Price writes, "conferences are often among the least accessible spaces that people with disabilities encounter in the course of our work, since they combine the typical inaccessibility of public spaces with the fact that most participants are on unfamiliar ground" ("Access Imagined"). And yet, scholars of all levels, from graduate students to senior scholars, are expected to present their research consistently at conferences. This expectation puts disabled scholars in the uncomfortable situation of choosing between navigating potentially unfamiliar and inaccessible spaces or missing out on opportunities to network and further develop their research projects—and thus their careers.

For the authors of the CCCC Accessibility Guides, writing the guides can be a way to confront the overwhelming inaccessibility of conference experiences by compiling and delivering access information to anyone who wants it. The guides work to flip the script on access; so often, access is framed as an individual responsibility, with the burden placed on the disabled person to request accommodations from the organization. Critical access literacies, informed by disability justice principles, envision access as a collective responsibility, one in which everyone is committed to moving "together as people with mixed abilities, multi-racial, multi-gendered, mixed class, across the orientation spectrum – where no body/mind is left behind" (Sins Invalid 19). Lauren Cagle frames her work on the 2015 CCCC Accessibility Guide as redistributing access labor and countering oppressive structures:

> We hoped that we could produce something that would free up time and space for people to engage in the other kinds of self-advocacy they might need to do. [...] [The guide] changes the discourse around this event more broadly but in a very specific individual level. We want to take action to enable other people to save themselves time and energy. Because so often that's what we demand of disabled people just to exist in the world. [...] We demand their time and energy, and that's oppressive. It's oppressive. There's no way around it.

Cagle describes the critical function of the access literacies practiced in the guide: by consolidating and sharing access knowledge, guide authors counter oppressive frameworks of disability that demand disabled scholars devote time and energy to simply exist in the conference space. Rather than placing the responsibility on individual CCCC members with disabilities to find essential access information on their own, the existence of the guides argues that sharing access knowledge is a collective responsibility.

By consolidating access information from various sources about various needs and various spaces, the accessibility guides act as a resource hub for disabled CCCC members. Because the guide authors didn't have the power to actually alter the conference venue layout to be more accessible, they envision the information-sharing of critical access literacies as a move toward collective access. As Cobos explains, "I couldn't change the space. I couldn't change the carpet, for example, but I could give people a heads up: 'hey, this carpet is busy or not busy. Here's what it looks like or here's a description of what it looks like.'" While the guide authors are limited in what they are able to do to enact access on a physical level, they also recognize the importance of alerting conference-goers to the obstacles so that they can plan ahead of time. To that end, the 2011-2016 accessibility guides included information about transportation to and around the conference city, basic information about the conference venue – such as the carpet pattern for those with sensory needs –, basic information about the conference hotel – such as the availability of wheelchair accessible hotel rooms –, and local restaurants that accommodate different dietary restrictions.

Walter recalls disabled scholars thanking her, saying, "having the guide online – this is helpful to be able to see this information before I got here.'" Though the information in the guide might initially appear benign – it's often written in a neutral tone that doesn't condemn the accessibility obstacles it identifies – Cobos' and Cagle's reflections illustrate how providing this information gives disabled scholars the ability to prepare for the space, and free up spoons[6] for engaging with the conference experience. Thus, the guide is a tool for resisting ableism, a way for volunteers – both disabled and nondisabled – to share the load of ensuring access.

Because CCCC distributes the accessibility guide to all conference-goers through emails, social media, and the conference website, the information is theoretically circulated beyond disabled scholars who identify as needing this information. By speaking about disability access to a general audience, the accessibility guides invoke the pedagogical potential of critical access literacies. While disabled CCCC members were the priority, they were not the only intended audience. As Dolmage explained in our Skype interview,

> I think there's another group of people who didn't necessarily think they'd use [the guide] but now really do use it because it just becomes a good way to navigate—thinking through where they're going, what the space is like for a wide variety of reasons.

Many of the guides' authors echoed Dolmage, expressing that they wanted their guide to be useful for people who did not necessarily identify as disabled. One of goals in creating the guide was to "speak to as many different people who might be reading that guide for as many different reasons as they might be." All of the guides I studied included information that might not initially seem disability-focused, and thus, be seen as more general interest:

- Price's 2011 guide included information about local attractions with notes about crowded each can be.
- Walter's 2012 guide directed attendees on how to find quiet meeting spaces at a conference hotel
- Dolmage's 2013 guide describes the inconsistent length of city blocks on the Las Vegas strip
- Donhardt's 2014 guide alerts readers that the marble floor of the conference venue becomes slippery when wet
- Cagle and Browing's 2015 guide lists the locations of two pharmacies close to the conference venue
- Cobos and Canino's 2016 guide identified free recreational activities close to the conference venue

Though these references did not mention disability explicitly, the accessibility guide writers understood these all as access issues. The ability to find a quiet space is key for some people with mental disabilities (Anglesey and Cecil-Lemkin) but also people who just need a place to collect their thoughts or read messages from home without interruption. The location of nearby pharmacies could be crucial information for people with chronic illness but also people in need of over-the-counter remedies for headaches or seasonal allergies.

The guide authors centered disability in the guides while imagining a broader audience, so as to include everyone in the mission of creating access. Walter calls this the "mantra of accessibility," invoking a core principle of Universal Design: "if things are as inclusive as they can be in regards to disability, they're as inclusive as it can be for everybody." Universal Design rhetoric has been recently critiqued for erasing disability in its focus on the universal (Hamraie *Building* 7). The accessibility guides navigate that critique by speaking about access expansively to a wide audience while also naming and identifying barriers specific to disabled people. In this way, critical access literacies, like other forms of literacy, are pedagogical. The guide serves as an educational text, informing both nondisabled and disabled conference-goers about the diverse and various needs of disabled scholars. Cagle observes that each time the guide is released, people discuss it on social media: "My sense is that the online conversation . . . around disability, accessibility has become bigger. And also there are people who get involved in that conversation who wouldn't necessarily have before." Cagle believes that the guide's presence sparks a conversation among conference-goers about access and disability. Thus, more broadly, the authors of accessibility guides invite conference goers, even those outside of disability studies, to develop critical access literacies by teaching them how to identify access issues and talk about disability access.

The critical access literacies of the guides also serve an argumentative function: by attempting to make the conference experience accessible for disabled scholars, the guides argue for the value of disabled wisdom. As discussed earlier, academic conferences have historically been exclusive and even hostile to disabled scholars. Such overwhelming and constant inaccessibility sends a message to disabled scholars: you are not welcome here. The Accessibility Guide combats that messaging by asserting that disabled scholars are valued members of the community. Walter insists, "just doing [the guide] every year for the conference makes a statement to the organization: this is important and this is something that matters." Walter highlights the rhetorical power of critical access literacies: the guides assert that disabled scholars have something vital to contribute to the profession, and thus, deserve access to conferences. Critical access literacies cultivate an awareness that disabled people exist, that they are often excluded, and that institutions should make an active effort to include and affirm them. And such awareness extends beyond how CCCC operates. Cobos recalls conversations with CCCC members about the guide's impact outside of the conference: "people said, 'this would be really useful to have at my school because we don't think about some of these things.' Others said, 'this has challenged me in how I think about my students and how can I change the classroom setting.'" The culture shift is not necessarily limited to just the conference space of CCCC, then. As the authors and interpreters develop critical access literacies through their engagement with the guide, they are able to transfer those literacies to other spaces. Given that CCCC focuses on the teaching of writing, the guide presents an exciting opportunity to prompt CCCC members to consider how they can bring critical access literacies on their campuses and in their classrooms.

Over the years, the guides expanded because of increased content and the incorporation of images and captions. This expansion has allowed the guides to highlight the intersectional aspect of access, a key Disability Justice principle. As several disability studies scholars and justice activists have argued, access knowledge that focuses solely on disability only focuses on the access needs of white disabled cisgender men (Hubrig and Osorio 94). An intersectional approach to access prompts us to consider how different raced, gendered, nationed, and other Othered disabled bodies navigate a space. 2015 marked a significant year in the evolution of the guide, especially in its focus on intersectional access. Powered by a full committee of volunteers and greater institutional support from CCCC, the 2015 guide became a more dynamic, interactive genre, including photographs and captions as well as more extensive access information. Browning explains, "we were trying to really give as much information as we could about the conference sites and where folks were going to be going potentially and speak to as many different people who might be reading that guide for as many different reasons as they might be." The 2015 guide spoke to various disability access needs, including extensive photographs and descriptions of the pool lifts in the conference hotel, carpet patterns (for people with sensory needs), and building entrances. In addition, the guide provided information on how to find gender neutral bathrooms, how to find the lactation space, where and when to find Alcoholics Anonymous and Narcotics Anonymous meetings. Thus, the guide provides critical access information addressing the needs of trans scholars, nursing parents, and folks dealing with addiction. Disability rarely operates in isolation of other identities. As the performer-activists of Sins Invalid explain, "each person has multiple identities, and each identity can be a site of privilege or oppression" (16). Disabled people have babies, they need gender neutral bathrooms, they deal with drug addiction. The CCCC Accessibility Guides I studied do not address race explicitly, so there are intersectional access needs that are overlooked. Still, in 2015, the CCCC Accessibility Guides began to overtly recognize that disabled people occupy different types of bodies and live different types of lives, and thus might need intersectional forms of access.

Cobos and Canino followed Cagle and Browning's lead by also including material about gender neutral bathrooms, lactation spaces, and NA/AA meetings in the 2016 CCCC Accessibility Guide. In addition, they included a list of free recreational activities in the conference city, which Cobos explains in our interview was a response to the high cost of conferences. Cobos hopes that future CCCC organizers and guide authors will "make sure this conference is not just for the people with money and faculty who have tenure track jobs." The Free Fun and Relaxation section of the 2016 guide identifies "things [people] can do on a budget to improve [their] conference experience" (38). By framing finances as an access concern, the 2016 Accessibility Guide emphasizes that the high costs can be barriers to access. Class intersects with disability in profound ways, as disabled people live in poverty "at twice the rate of people without disabilities" (National Council on Disability). While Cobos couldn't control the cost of conference registration or travel, she *could* frame cost as an access issue. Cobos, Canino, Cagle, and Browning all demonstrate the importance of integrating an intersectional awareness in critical access literacies. They understand that trans, nursing, and poor disabled people need dynamic and multilayered access to participate in knowledge-sharing at CCCC.

As accessibility guides have become more and more commonplace in writing studies, other conferences in the field have incorporated them and built upon the foundation of the early CCCC guide writers. In 2018, the Rhetoric Society of America (RSA) conference offered an accessibility guide, authored by Stephanie Larson. The guide included similar information as the early CCCC guides, but Larson also included a tribal welcome and land acknowledgment early in the guide. Katie Bramlett followed this practice for the 2019 RSA Institute, and I did as well for the 2019 Mid-Atlantic CCCC Conference at ODU, adding a slavery acknowledgment and a note for those observing Ramadan. These more explicit references to colonialism and race within the context of accessibility illustrate the potential for foregrounding intersectionality in critical access literacies. I read these inclusions in accessibility guides as a recognition that colonialism and racist violence are themselves sources of disability, frailty, and trauma. The ongoing threat of state violence against Black and Indigenous people *is* an access issue, as it impedes the free movement of minoritized people targeted by white supremacy. This is a place in need of further expansion in future CCCC Access Guides; information about local policing and immigration policies, for instance, can enable BIPOC and undocumented CCCC members to make decisions about how or if to navigate the conference city.

Despite the ability of access guides to attend to disability access, they are limited in how much they can transform an academic organization. Friend, colleague, and co-conspirator Margaret Fink once asked me, "can academia, with its love of productivity, efficiency, and its investments in gatekeeping, ever truly embody Disability Justice principles?" This question has stuck with me since. After all, DJ is inherently an anti-capitalist, anti-settler project. The accessibility guides themselves illustrate this tension between the activists' attempt to enact radical access and the institutional barriers to such transformation. While the guides' authors overwhelmingly articulated that the guide has helped to change CCCC culture, some also noted the limitations of the guide in enacting true structural transformation. As Cobos stated, she didn't have the authority to physically change the space or lower registration costs to make the conference more accessible. Dolmage echoes this frustration and goes further in our interview: the guide *allows* CCCC to continue choosing inaccessible spaces. He explains, "[The guide] may need to become a little bit more political. I think we may need to be thinking about the fact that we can't keep just using the guide to cover for the inaccessible spaces CCCC chooses." Earlier in our conversation, Dolmage noted the *cultural* changes within CCCC since 2011, such as increased participation in the Disability Studies Standing Group meeting. However, he also insists that the institution itself still does not prioritize accessibility in its conference planning. If it were to, he argues, it would make accessibility a core concern in choosing venues. But ultimately, cost is prioritized over accessibility, suggesting the accessibility guides serve more as a Band-Aid for inaccessibility than a true transformation.

Because the guide authors are often disabled, the guides also threaten to further burden disabled people and their accomplices with additional access labor. In our interview, Price discusses the lack of institutional memory and support faced by the guide authors:

> There is sort of this constant tension between we're the ones who do access best (we being the disabled people and members of the CDICC), and yet every time we do this and do a great job, CCCC is unsurprisingly like, "great thanks!" We don't necessarily want that to be our role. That's an organizational responsibility. So I think that's led to problems with whether people doing the work are getting enough support.

Price and Dolmage observe that professional organizations often rely on volunteer labor to point out accessibility issues instead of embedding accessibility into organization's structure. Their observations underscore the challenges of practicing critical access literacies in professional spaces that historically have disenfranchised and excluded disabled people. In her 2009 study of conference disability policy documents, Price asks, "if we wish to create accessible ways to meet one another and share our ideas, what traditions of competitiveness and agonistic discourse, of academic hierarchies in general, will have to be dismantled?" ("Access Imagined"). Price speaks to the fact that for disability liberation to occur, it can't just be the folks who study disability who commit to it: deep systemic change is needed, and our fundamental assumptions about the culture and structure of conferences need to change. All levels of academic institutions must commit to critical access literacy practices in order to construct communities that truly embrace the presence and wisdom of multiply marginalized disabled scholars.

Conclusion

I imagine this article making two interventions: the first is defining critical access literacies and analyzing a case study of them in action within a professional context. In doing this, I aim to highlight how critical access literacies can be practiced to dismantle ableist structures while building a world for disability liberation. Despite the limitations of the Accessibility Guides, all the authors I spoke to believe in the power of the guides to transform culture in CCCC. Price recalls feeling, "It's so much work, but also hey! I'm really making a difference here. I'm really doing something that has a concrete good that I can look at and point to." By nature, Accessibility Guides are limited in what they can do, but they still are doing something by naming and valuing the presence of disability within CCCC. Vancouver's Radical Access Mapping Project (RAMP) speaks to the importance of auditing a space's access/lack of access:

> And while [an accessibility audit] isn't everything, doesn't do everything, doesn't encompass everything and isn't without its limitations, it does add something, it does create dialogue and tangible change. I've seen it, experi-

enced it firsthand. And in a society that is pretty consistently telling variously disabled folks that our presence doesn't have an impact, that our lives are not worth making and sharing space with, that does mean something.

Both Price and RAMP remind us that even when institutions overlook disabled people, communities can respond by cultivating material practices that facilitate belonging, community, and affirmation. Critical access literacies empower the composers and interpreters to be aware of the myriad and intersecting ways spaces can exclude disabled people, just as they also enable us to imagine a world built to embrace multiply marginalized disabled people.

The second intervention builds upon the first: by detailing the labor and the impact of Accessibility Guides, I hope that academic institutions begin valuing critical access literacy practices in meaningful, material, and sustainable ways. A study of the Accessibility Guides shows how, in spaces traditionally hostile to disability, critical access literacies can foster knowledge-making and knowledge-sharing about disability, intersectionality, and embodiment. Critical access literacies elevate traditional approaches to access communication, such as the Mid-Atlantic University's disability policy, that seek to fix "disability" and avoid litigation. When composed through a critical access literacy framework, disability policy documents can be sites of rich world-making. And yet, because conference accessibility guides are not peer-reviewed publications, their knowledge-building power can be overlooked by academic institutions – in particular, hiring and tenure and promotion committees. How can we rebuild our organizations to not just permit the existence of disabled people but actually value and center the work of creating access? How can we position critical access literacies as the heart of an organization, so that collective access is seen as a life force that enriches every aspect of that organization's work? I believe critical access literacies have the power to transform ableist cultures into disability liberated zones. To get us there in writing studies, our departments, universities, and professional organizations need to invest in the development of critical access literacies as something *we all* do rather than something *those people over there* do.

Notes

1. I would like to thank Margaret Price, Muffy Walter, Tracy Donhardt, Lauren Cagle, Ellie Browning, Casie Cobos, and Jay Dolmage for sharing their experiences of composing the Accessibility Guides with me and offering feedback throughout the writing and rewriting of this article in its many forms. I am grateful for Stephanie Kerschbaum's feedback on a very early draft of this project, as well as the reviewers and editors of this special issue.

2. The 2019 CCCC Accessibility Guide was written by John Grant, Ya-Huei Chen, and Noel Tague.

3. Geneva Canino is the other co-author of the 2016 Accessibility Guide for Houston; I was not able to interview Canino.

4. I sought and received permission from the interviewees to include their quotations in this article, and I offered each of them the opportunity to review the manuscript.

5. Inspired by J. Logan Smilges work on neuroqueer literacies, I am de-centering reading in my approach to literacies; as Smilges explains, "neuroqueer literacies are an intentional and strategic positioning of neurodivergent meaning-making practices in response to an ableist model of reading pedagogy that is predicated on the exclusion of disabled bodymind" (105). Thus, I use phrases like creating rather than writing and interpreting rather than reading, to encapsulate the various methods people use to interact with texts.

6. Christine Miserandino developed spoon theory as a metaphor for the units of energy disabled and sick people expend on day-to-day activities, emphasizing that disabled and sick people often have limited "spoons" to use in a day and have to strategically decide how to distribute their units of energy.

Works Cited

Anglesey, Leslie and Ellen Cecil-Lemkin. "The Importance of Keeping Conference Quiet Rooms Quiet." *College Composition and Communication*, vol. 72, no. 1, 2020, pp. 99-102.

Browning, Ellie. Skype Interview. 14 June 2017.

Cagle, Lauren and Ellie Browning. "CCCC 2015 Accessibility Guide: Tampa." CCCC, http://www.ncte.org/library/NCTEFiles/Groups/CCCC/Convention/2015/Accessibility-Guide.pdf. Accessed 12. Oct. 2017.

Cagle, Lauren. Skype Interview. 6 June 2017.

Cobos, Casie and Geneva Canino. "CCCC 2016 Accessibility Guide: Houston." CCCC, https://u.osu.edu/composingaccess/files/2016/09/2016-CCCC-Accessibility-Guide-2l9dewx.pdf. Accessed 12 Oct. 2017.

Cobos, Casie. Skype Interview. 12 June 2017.

Darnell Pritchard, Eric. *Fashioning Lives: Black Queers and the Politics of Literacy*. Southern Illinois University Press, 2017.

Dolmage, Jay. "Mapping Composition: Inviting Disability in the Front Door." *Disability and the Teaching of Writing: A Critical Sourcebook*, edited by Cynthia Lewiecki-Wilson and Brenda Brueggemann, Bedford/St. Martin, 2007, pp. 14-27.

—. Skype Interview. 15 June 2017.

— (uncredited). "CCCC 2013 Accessibility Guide: Las Vegas." CCCC. https://www.disabilityrhetoric.files.wordpress.com/cccc-2013-accessibility-guide-las-vegas-by-cdicc.doc. Accessed 12 Oct. 2017.

Donhardt, Tracy. "CCCC 2014 Accessibility Guide: Indianapolis." CCCC.

—. Phone Interview. 25 May 2017.

Flannery, Kathryn Thoms. *Feminist Literacies, 1968-75*. University of Illinois Press, 2010.

Fink, Margaret. Online Chat. 28 Feb. 2020.

Flowers, Linda. *Community Literacy and the Rhetoric of Public Engagement*. Southern Illinois University Press, 2008.

Hamraie, Aimi. *Building Access: Universal Design and the Politics of Disability*. U of Minnesota P, 2017.

—. "Making Access Critical: Disability, Race, and Gender in Environmental Design." Video Lecture given at Othering and Belonging Institute in Berkeley, CA, Feb. 25 2019. belonging.berkeley.edu/aimi-hamraie-making-access-critical-disability-race-and-gender-environmental-design.

Hubrig, Ada and Ruth Osorio. "Enacting a Culture of Access in Our Conference Spaces." *College Composition and Communication*, vol. 72, no. 1, 2020.

Kafai, Shayda. *Crip Kinship: The Disability Justice & Art Activism of Sins Invalid*. Arsenal Pulp Press, 2021.

Long, Elenore. *Community Literacy and the Rhetoric of Local Publics*. Parlor Press; The WAC Clearinghouse, 2008.

Luke, Allan. "Critical Literacy: Foundational Notes." *Theory into Practice*, vol. 51, no. 1, 2012, pp. 4–11.

Mingus, Mia, Alice Wong, Sandy Ho. "Access Is Love." *Disability Visibility Project*, 1 Feb. 2019, https://disabilityvisibilityproject.com/2019/02/01/access-is-love/. Accessed 14 Feb. 2020.

Mingus, Mia. "'Disability Justice' Is Simply Another Word for Love." Keynote Speech for 2018 Disability Intersectionality Summit. *Leaving Evidence*, 3 Nov. 2018, https://leavingevidence.wordpress.com/2018/11/03/disability-justice-is-simply-another-termforlove/. Accessed 25 Feb. 2020.

Miserandino, Christine. "The Spoon Theory." *But You Don't Look Sick*, 2003. https://butyoudontlooksick.com/articles/written-by-christine/the-spoon-theory/. Accessed 21 April 2022.

National Council on Disability. "Highlighting Disability / Poverty Connection, NCD Urges Congress to Alter Federal Policies that Disadvantage People with Disabilities." *NCD*, 26 October 2017, https://ncd.gov/newsroom/2017/disability-poverty-connection-2017-progress-report-release. Accessed 21 April 2022.

Piepzna-Samarasinha, Leah Lakshmi. *Care Work: Dreaming Disability Justice*. Arsenal Pulp P, 2018.

Powell, Malea. "Greetings from the 2011 Program Chair." *2011 CCCC Conference Program*. Accessed 21 April 2022, https://cccc.ncte.org/cccc/review/2011program.

Price, Margaret. "Access Imagined: The Construction of Disability in Conference Policy Documents." *Disability Studies Quarterly*, vol. 29, no. 1, Jan. 2009, doi:10.18061/dsq.v29i1.174.

—. "Accessibility Guide for Atlanta, GA." CCCC, 2011, margaretprice.files.wordpress.com/2011/01/atlanta-accessibility-guide-2011.pdf. Accessed. 12 Oct. 2017.

—. Phone Interview. 23 May 2017.

Radical Access Mapping Project. "On Really Getting What An Audit Is About." *RAMP*, 8 April 2015, https://radicalaccessiblecommunities.wordpress.com/2015/04/08/on-really-getting-what-an-audit-is-about/. Accessed 22 April 2022.

Richardson, Elaine. *African-American Literacies*. Taylor & Francis, 2003.

Sheridan-Rabideau, Mary P. *Girls, Feminism, and Grassroots Literacies*. State University of New York, 2008.

Sins Invalid. *Skin, Tooth, and Bone: The Basis of Movement Is Our People*. Sins Invalid, 2016.

Smilges, Logan J. "Neuroqueer Literacies; or, Against Able-Reading." *College Composition and Communication*, vol. 73, no. 1, 2021, pp. 103-125.

Titchkosky, Tanya. *The Question of Access: Disability, Space, Meaning*. U of Toronto P, 2011.

Walter, Muffy. "CCCC 2012 Accessibility Guide: St. Louis." CCCC. http://www.ncte.org/library/nctefiles/groups/cccc/convention/2012/cccc2012accessibilityguide.pdf. Accessed 12 Oct. 2017.

—. Phone Interview. 31 May 2017.

Yergeau, Remi M. "Saturday Plenary Address: Creating a Culture of Access in Writing Program Administration." *WPA: Writing Program Administration*, vol. 40, no. 1, 2016, pp. 155-65.

Appendix A: Interview Questions

1. What was your role in the crafting of the accessibility guide? How did the Accessibility Coordinator work with the Local Arrangements Committee?
2. Can you describe the behind-the-scenes labor that crafting this guide required? Who did the work and how was the labor delegated?
3. What was your guiding philosophy when crafting the accessibility guide? What did you want to emphasize and why?
4. Did you experience any challenges in creating the guide, and how did you overcome them?
5. What role did CCCC as an organization have in directing your work with the guide? What kind of support or feedback did they provide?
6. To what extent do you see creating the accessibility guide as activism?
7. To what extend has the CCCC Accessibility Guide changed the culture of CCCC in terms of disability awareness and justice?
8. What kind of service credits or recognition, if any, did you receive from your department for developing the guide?
9. Do you have anything else to add?

Author Bio

Ruth Osorio is an Assistant Professor of English and Women's Studies at Old Dominion University, where she teaches classes on feminist rhetorical studies, feminist disability studies, and composition. Her research on disability and activism has appeared in *College English, enculturation,* and *CCC*. When she isn't writing or teaching, she's hanging out with her family, playing with her dog, or reading novels.

Storying Access: Citizen Journalism, Disability Justice, and the Kansas City Homeless Union

Brynn Fitzsimmons

Abstract

This article is an ethnographic case study of the work of two activist groups in Kansas City, Missouri. It discusses how unhoused activists with the Kansas City Homeless Union, through their 13-month on-and-off occupation of city property, worked to reframe access in ways that moved toward what disability justice activists call collective access, prioritized marginalized lived experience, and asserted their right to control over the resources that impacted their lives. This article ties these interventions explicitly to community writing work through a discussion of how citizen journalists from Independent Media Association, with whom the author has collaborated, documented and crafted narratives around the union's work in ways that demonstrate ways community literacy work can function as rhetorical solidarity practices.

Keywords

Disability justice, access, citizen journalism, housing rights, community writing, abolition

Content Warning: brief discussions of suicide and police brutality

Introduction

On New Year's Day in 2021, during the coldest, most brutal snowstorm of the year, Sixx, a Black unhoused[1] man, was found naked and frozen to death in the snow in Kansas City, Missouri. The day before, protesters had gathered outside the Kansas City mayor's residence at the start of a snowstorm and cold spell that proved the worst of the year so far. The same abolitionist protesters who had, back in October, demanded that the $273 million police budget be cut in half and reinvested in "life-affirming institutions," including housing, now extended their call to action, calling for immediate housing solutions for Kansas City's growing unhoused population (Stoica, December 31).[2] The city did not respond—and then came news reports from multiple stations that Sixx had died.

Less than a week later, I was on the phone doing interviews with his family for citizen journalism project Independent Media Association (IMA)—a group with which I have worked closely since fall of 2020. While news outlets were talking about Sixx's death, IMA's hope was for a story that was about Sixx's life as well. What we ultimately ran was somewhere in between a news story and a long obituary, and, importantly, citizen journalists were the *only* journalists Sixx's family ever talked to, even though dozens of news stories would run his photo alongside work being done in his name. Sixx's story, like many stories of unhoused individuals IMA would publish after that, included passing references to disability–in Sixx's case, to lingering effects of childhood trauma, mental health needs around communication and interpersonal relationships that went unmet, injuries that caused him to lose scholarships and thus never finish school–and the ways in which many services harmed rather than helped (see Fitzsimmons, "In Memoriam"). Sixx's family, like many others, also spoke of camp sweeps—where city employees, usually from Parks and Recreation, give written and thus often inaccessible notice for residents of a camp to leave and then bulldoze anything remaining at the camp 48 hours later—as one of the most violent forms of "help" available to unhoused communities. That story was the beginning of far too many stories I and other citizen journalists from IMA would write, livestream, photograph, and video that began and ended at "access" with strings attached, and shelters that look like prisons. And right from the beginning, Sixx's story drew what would become an increasingly important distinction in discourse around houselessness in Kansas City: "solutions" that were not self-determined by unhoused people—especially those most at risk, which includes disabled houseless people—almost always caused more harm than good. Even the best-intentioned state solutions didn't save Sixx or the many others like him—and that, citizen journalists quickly found, had to be the story.

Sixx's death shook the city. Activists who had never worked on direct services for houseless people jumpstarted warming centers, began negotiating with city council for funding and space in community centers, and joined new city taskforces on houselessness. Organizations like Free Hot Soup, a direct-services mutual aid group whose members had known Sixx well, redoubled their efforts and expanded their volunteer base. They joined with Creative Innovative Entrepreneurs, a nonprofit which had up until that point served at-risk youth ages 16-21, to open and help staff the Scott Eicke Warming Center—named for Sixx.[3] Meanwhile, Qadhafi, a Black, homeless, formerly incarcerated man who had been working with housing rights group KC Tenants, called a meeting among the homeless camps and proposed a homeless union. The group elected him leader and established the Kansas City Homeless Union (KCHU), whose first action was to occupy city hall in protest. While activists ran the warming center and, later, other activists collaborated with unhoused individuals to run Camp Sixx, a camp in Westport, KCHU was decided in their position. Homelessness, they said, would be addressed through access to "homes, jobs, water, and a seat at the table," and decisions would be by and for homeless people—not housed city officials, nonprofits, or even activists. Qadhafi said his goal was to "make homelessness the number one issue"—and, over the next year, he did (March 23).

Storying Access

How do we—community writing practitioners, both academic and non-academic—story access at the intersection of disability and abolition? What and for whom does it matter that we do? This article considers these questions of how we story access by looking at two different threads of the story sketched above: the work of citizen journalists at IMA, an abolitionist, Kansas City-based citizen journalism project, and the work of the all unhoused-led KCHU, predominantly as documented by IMA citizen journalists, both because their coverage is the most extensive and because they/we were, eventually, the only media outlet to keep covering. Both IMA and KCHU deal directly with questions of access to news and housing, respectively. However, examining their work through a disability justice lens also clarifies linkages between disability and abolition, particularly in community literacy contexts.

As QTBIPOC writers like Leah Lakshmi Piepzna-Samarasinha point out, we cannot understand disability justice without abolition, and our movements will likewise not be healing and life-affirming without disability justice (Piepzna-Samarasinha 83-96). This is true for those doing community writing work, as IMA and KCHU did, both inside and outside the academy. However, community literacy work as a *practice* of collective, liberatory access that undoes the white supremacist, colonial systems that created inaccessibility to begin with is perhaps particularly important for scholar-activists to consider (see Dolmage; Mingus; Sins Invalid). White disabled academics like me do a lot of talking about intersectionality while practicing complicity with white supremacist, settler colonial, carceral logics, and so how we show up in activist movements and policy changes—including movements built on the labor of disabled QTBIPOC—tends to reinforce those systems. For example, as someone who is white and grew up with class privilege in the Midwest, I often felt the pull to look at church-, nonprofit-, and advocate-run projects as well-intentioned and on the right track—to not be too critical because "at least they're trying." But as KCHU leader Qadhafi pointed out repeatedly, the best intentions did not erase that "a shelter is only in the business of capitalizing off of us being homeless," (qtd. in Fitzsimmons, "We Are Not Accidentally Homeless"). In other words, access to homes, or jobs, or other services without self-determination and the abolition of systems and logics that strip people of self-determination isn't really access. Nor can we end houselessness with academia's ever-more-rigorous critique; critiques don't house people.

White scholars in particular, by buying into what la paperson terms the "second university's" assertion that analysis and critique are in themselves liberatory or decolonizing work are particularly guilty of reifying these systems (41-43). Instead, la paperson pushes us to think about a third, decolonizing university that turns colonial systems against themselves–a small piece of which I hope to parse out here by considering how community literacy projects like IMA can materially amplify KCHU's abolitionist repositioning of what access *is* and what we *do* about it in the context of housing. Specifically, in this article, I consider how KCHU and the citizen journalists who most extensively covered their activism story that kind of liberatory access, what it looks like to center knowledges and leadership of those most impacted, and how citizen journalism as a community writing/media project is perhaps uniquely suited to do that work.

As scholarship like Liat Ben-Moshe's *Decarcerating Disability* has pointed out, and abolitionists like Angela Davis, Gina Dent, Erica Meiners, and Beth Ritchie have recently affirmed, disability justice and abolition are intimately connected. The decarceration of mentally and physically disabled people between 1977 and 2015 was in part possible because of changing media narratives that, while they fell short of a full critique of carceral logics, still shifted public opinion from seeing the institutionalization of disabled people as necessary to understanding institutions like asylums and other facilities as inhuman and dehumanizing (Ben-Moshe 3-4; 46-53). However, the logic that some bodily difference is so dangerous that it must be segregated and expunged persists, often marginalizing and incarcerating disabled people, particularly disabled people of color (Annamma 7; Price 166-173). Carceral logics also cast body-based categories like sexuality and gender as so rigidly hierarchized that they are, themselves, carceral (Smith 5-6)—something scholars of disability and mad studies note as often true of the categorization of disability (Cherney; Puar) as well as true of medical and psychiatric institutions and knowledge (Ben-Moshe; Kafer; Piepzna-Samarasinha; Price). At a macro-level, in many ways, prisons and police continue to be imaginable because body-based discrimination—what activist Sonya Renee Taylor calls "body terrorism" (54)—is imaginable, and ableism is often one of the justifications for gendered and racialized violence (Schalk, Bailey, Bailey and Peoples). Thus, while the activist work from both unhoused activists and citizen journalists that I consider here is not directly engaging disability—housing rights, abolition, and media freedom are more common ways for these activists to situate their work—a large dimension of their work against carceral logics or toward access and body-based justice become clearer through a disability justice lens.

The way access specifically is positioned in these examples of activist media is, I argue, *storying* work. In calling this "storying," I hope to invoke the varied forms of storytelling that get at power, where it lies, whom it harms, and how to dismantle it in favor of a world built on collective access, mutual aid, and liberation (see Kafer; Sins Invalid). For example, M. Remi Yergeau uses "storying" as method in *Authoring Autism* to resist erasure and control through an intentional retelling of other people's narratives of one's bodymind. They deploy this method throughout their book as a way of narrativizing dominant narratives of autism through a neuroqueer lens—to assert the authority of their own experience and tease out the points at which that lived experience disproves dominant, ableist narratives, exposes them as violent, and renders them untenable.

Although the work activists and citizen journalists are doing takes a different form than Yergeau's book, I argue the storying work is fundamentally similar. Unhoused activists regularly engaged, retold, and exposed as violent the city's and the media's narratives of homelessness in Kansas City—stories that often involve, even if it is not explicitly stated, both physical and mental disability. Relatedly, IMA's methods of citizen journalism engaged dominant narratives only to filter them through the lens of people's lived experience, a choice which shaped their reporting from the outset of KCHU's occupation and, importantly, kept them reporting on that work long after other media outlets gave up.

This conception of storytelling as a way of exposing systems of power and working to dismantle them is found in other areas of storytelling as a critical methodology as well; perhaps most notably in critical race theory's *counterstory*, which Aja Martinez discusses as "exposing stereotypes and injustice and offering additional truths through a narration of the researchers' own experiences," (17). By storying access via the lived experience of those who are being denied access, unhoused activists and citizen journalists intervened in how access is defined; resisting, for example, the idea that more surveillance or control can ever create access to safe and healthy communities. Unhoused activists in Kansas City demanded self-determination—moving, over the course of their 13-month occupation, toward resetting the terms of discussions about access to housing that were determined by unhoused people, not city agendas. In focusing on storying access, citizen journalists worked to advance these terms—to create a media narrative that advanced both epistemic justice and collective, liberatory access.

"Every Damn Body": The Kansas City Homeless Union Occupation

Just days after IMA published Sixx's story, Andrei Stoica, the founder of IMA, met and began talking with Qadhafi, who was heading the KCHU occupation on city hall front lawn, demanding "homes, jobs, water, and a seat at the table". KCHU staged an on and off occupation of Kansas City, Missouri city property for a year, before their camp was destroyed by city officials who said they moved everyone into some kind of housing and then bulldozed the camp to turn it into a dog park. There were countless "sweep threats" (see March 23, April 5) before then—times the camp had been given notice to vacate under threat of being bulldozed—and IMA showed up alongside protesters with livestream cameras. City officials claimed sweeps were not violent and that people's property and homes were not destroyed. Among other interventions, the city gave additional money to shelters as well as new groups claiming they were addressing houselessness. However, unhoused individuals–many of whom told their stories on IMA's livestream cameras while we all waited for threatened sweeps–told a different story. Specifically, when KCHU activists, whether on their own channels or on IMA's livestreams, described sweeps and other city responses to unhoused communities, they talked about how the only "access" offered by the city came with strings attached–like shelters with strict surveillance or rules that banned the majority of unhoused folx on the basis of sexuality, previous criminal records, or disability (March 23).

In an interview Andrei eventually ran a transcript of on IMA's website, Qadhafi talked about the importance of forcing elected officials to *see* their unhoused constituents (Stoica, "My Address Is"). As Qadhafi would continue to repeat for the next year of on and off occupation, "to be seen is to be heard." In so doing, they asked for a reframing of the city's sense of accountability to its constituents, asking questions not dissimilar to what Cody A. Jackson and Christina V. Cedillo asked the field of rhetoric and composition in their 2020 article: "If accountability ends at the mention of "structural" issues, how can we reframe accountability politics as a profoundly localized, embodied endeavor (Mingus "Dreaming Accountability")?" Unhoused activists sought to embody the citywide calls for accountability and access. These calls had started with Sixx, with his body, but had done little more than that second-university critique that la paperson discusses. These quickly faded into vague calls for change and vaguer promises for "help" as defined not by unhoused folx, but by people with power and 501c3 status. The union took a strong position from the start on this issue—intent on not settling for any less than self-determination.

Early in the occupation, Qadhafi described his work in the following way: "My job is to make every damn body uncomfortable and to make homelessness the number one issue," (March 23). It strikes me as important that his choice in emphasis splits the word: "every damn body". Qadhafi's strategy was for the union to be seen, and in so doing to hold the city accountable. To do so, he put a camp that would normally be tucked away out of sight right in front of city hall–which, in Kansas City, also means it was in front of the police department headquarters and the county courthouse, with a parking garage on the fourth side. He was determined that, in seeing bodies, he would make those with power uncomfortable enough that they would have to recognize the union–a tactic which worked, at least partially, in the sense that city officials did ultimately come down and meet with the union. Cedillo writes, "Those whose bodies are seen (in terms of surveillance and an ableist predilection for sight) as Other are framed as too corporeal and incapable of legitimate speech, as rhetorically expedient but never rhetorical in their own right. They are mere bodies, objects upon which meaning can be imposed," (n.p.), and Qadhafi's demand for "a seat at the table where they make decisions about our lives" (qtd. in Fitzsimmons, "We Are Not Accidentally Homeless") was precisely a resistance to this kind of imposition.

While city officials insisted throughout the KCHU occupation–in city council meetings, on IMA's camera, and to activists' faces–that sweeps were not violent and unhoused folx were able to move with their belongings into a shelter before a camp was "cleaned," that narrative was repeatedly combatted by anyone who actually experienced a sweep. Many unhoused folx and their housed friends sharing—with IMA citizen journalists and on their own social media channels—photo after photo of belongings bulldozed into a pile at the edge of what had once been a camp. In addition to detailing what sweeps looked like (see Fitzsimmons "In Memoriam"), homeless leaders also described the mental health impacts, such as Qadhafi noting after a sweep that one man from the camp "was so tired and constantly frustrated of being tried to run off that he tried to kill himself," (September 22), or talking about families panicking at the mere mention of a shelter, terrified that their children would be taken from them if they were judged unfit to be parents (March 23).

These stories–which are common among houseless communities outside of Kansas City as well–illustrate what Maya Schenwar and Victoria Law describe as the ever-expanding nature of the prison industrial complex via "almost-imprisonment... institutions that do not bear that name (prison) but are still Somewhere Else–places designed to cut off marginalized people from society," (20-21). This includes, for

Schenwar and Law, psychiatric institutions, foster care, the sex offender registry, probation, and a number of other systems that all also directly or indirectly impact homeless communities. As both their work and that of Qadhafi highlight, abolition of carceral institutions without the creation of liberatory access ends in more prisons *and* "services" that aren't called prisons but function in much the same way.

KCHU was an exercise in creating that kind of collective access that resisted extensions of state control. This emphasis was perhaps clearest about eight months into the occupation, when the camp had moved to city-owned property a few blocks away while city taskforces continued to pour money into service organizations–without substantively recognizing the authority of the union. In a September 22 interview, Qadhafi explained that people were leaving city-funded shelters and coming to the KCHU camp because "the city is feeding (shelters) money, but they (unhoused folx) don't want to be there. It's more like prison," Qadhafi described. "Here they're free." And from that place of freedom, Qadhafi invited Kansas City publics into a different kind of project: "If anything, we're gonna set the table and maybe invite them, because they're not the ones suffering and dying out here—it's us. So the table is amongst us, not us amongst them, because they're gonna continue doing the same thing and there's not going to be different results," (September 22). In other words, he pushed for, essentially, the same interdependence and cross-movement solidarity Sins Invalid calls crucial to disability justice–because he sees it as crucial to building power that threatens oppressive systems ("10 Principles"):

> The anarchists, abolitionists, anybody should get our back because we're proving we can do something that people only talk about or study, and we're proving that we can do it and do it without funds. And that's scary, I know it is, it's got to be, because (if) people continue to do this and come together and create autonomous communities…what we end up doing is creating autonomous neighborhoods and creating treaties between (camps) and creating our own federation—yeah, that's scary. You know, autonomous, life-affirming community. (September 22)

In addition to cross-movement solidarity, what Qadhafi presented here was abolition–it was a model of the "radical, life-affirming infrastructure and support along with a flowing stream of resources (which) is what creates safe, secure, healthy, sustainable and equitable communities, conditions that allow us to not only survive but thrive," which Critical Resistance discusses as the necessary alternative to carceral institutions. That includes prisons—but also, as Qadhafi points out, includes shelters and other parts of the non-profit industrial complex. It is access founded in both self-determination—camps are self-determined or autonomous here; and interdependence—camps working together to threaten the systems that marginalize them.

Self-determination—particularly within discourse around disability—has often been framed in terms that imply that the right to determine one's own life is a matter of gaining the right to be included in public institutions and discourses on the basis of individual independence that one earns by performing as a normative member of society, a normalization project that is closely linked to colonial projects (Ben-Moshe

79-80). However, KCHU reframed self-determination as the ability to use one's lived experience and the experiences of one's community to make decisions about the flow of resources that most directly impact one's life—as many abolitionist and anticolonial movements have framed self-determination (Stanley 90). While self-determination as defined in the neoliberal, colonial sense focuses on moving people toward proximity to hegemonic identities—e.g., performing able-bodied/able-mindedness, whiteness, masculinity, etc.—self-determination as KCHU used it is more centered on epistemic justice. That is, it is centered on addressing the asymmetrical ways in which credibility of knowledges, particularly embodied knowledges, and testimonies are assigned. In reframing unhoused speakers as able to self-determine the solutions that made sense to their communities, they worked to center how people–particularly disabled people, like many in the camp—make access via new and accessible systems, systems that, in the spirit of mutual aid, allow them to meet each other's needs in ways that, as Qadhafi sketches here, threaten the very systems that created that need to begin with.

Cripping Citizen Journalism

Although the camp began with a demand for "a seat at the table," KCHU eventually moved away from that. Instead, Qadhafi and other union leaders began saying they were creating their own table—calling explicitly for that later in the fall, and, even after the camp was ultimately swept by the city in February 2022, building toward those ends. It's here that the sources I've drawn on to this point matter. With few exceptions, the documentation of Qadhafi's and other unhoused activists' speeches comes from the work of IMA citizen journalists, and while the preceding section demonstrates some of the ways KCHU reframes access—what it means, who leads it, and what its material impacts look like—the way citizen journalists responded and used their/our writing to support not only fell in line with their dedication to information access (see "Who We Are," *Independent Media Association*), but it also illustrates a few ways community writing projects can and do support, amplify, and *story* radical, liberatory access.

Citizen journalism work is generally predicated on some concept of access to information, with citizen journalists often getting into their work because of a perceived *lack* of access to relevant, contextualized information in mainstream forms of news (see Allan, Allan and Thorson, and Greer and McLaughlin). Although most citizen journalism in the U.S. has historically been assumed right-leaning, citizen journalists—particularly those like IMA who do livestream coverage of protests, such as around the Ferguson and George Floyd uprisings—citizen journalists have played important roles in leftist movements as well (see Borda and Marshall). Having emerged from Kansas City's uprisings following the murder of George Floyd in 2020, IMA undertakes their citizen journalism work from an explicitly abolitionist lens, seeking to trouble carceral logics tied up in both "journalist" and "citizen" through open-access news that prioritizes lived experiences, challenging, as abolition does, "social logics and institutionalized systems of violence" (Rodriguez 810) through stories that expose impacts of state violence on actual people. Following Black feminist standpoint epistemology as articulated by writers like Patricia Hill Collins and bell hooks, IMA centers their coverage on lived experience of those most impacted by a given issue, their accounts, and their solutions.

I met Andrei Stoica, the founder of IMA, in September 2020, at a park outside a school before a Black Lives Matter protest. An acquaintance had introduced us via email after I'd had a bad health flare that was quickly slowing my capacity to show up in-person for protests; I started asking people if they needed a researcher or a writer. Andrei did. He was a photographer, and told me he had started IMA to livestream, photograph, and, he hoped, write about activist work following damaging media mis-coverage of 2020's protests and related events. For him, the final straw had been a local station—KCTV5—reporting that someone threw a pig's head at police. He had been there, and he doubted the accuracy of the story. He pulled together social media footage, eyewitness accounts, and photographs, all of which disproved KCTV5's story. He posted his documentation for his fact check publicly, sent it to them, and posted it as a comment on their story, which they never updated.

This hadn't been a one-off issue, either; news coverage of the 2020 protests tended to be like KCTV5's—centered on sensational headlines and photos, overly concerned with whether the police were good or bad, whether the protesters were violent or nonviolent, whether they had broken the law or obeyed all of them perfectly. People got ignored in those binaries. Meyerhoff and Noterman argue, "Reclaiming the university for projects of Black liberation and decolonization requires jettisoning this modernist/colonial (zero-point) epistemology in favor of place-and-body political epistemologies and alternative modes of study" (226). However, dominant media narratives, even if they talk about things like community-based safety, investing in housing or healthcare, or alternatives to policing, never really make it to that "place-and-body" epistemology either; they never trouble "dichotomies of 'human vs. animal,' 'society vs. nature,' and 'space vs. time'" (226) or, I would add, law and order vs. crime. By continuing to tell stories that replicate binaries that allow fundamentally violent systems to be one side of two acceptable options, mainstream news risks reifying carceral logics even as it claims to be covering interrogations of them.

For IMA, the carceral logics of the news such as the capitalist business models, economic and educational gatekeeping of journalism school, and sensationalist plays into dehumanizing algorithms do more than make *imaginable* the need for police, prisons, modern-day slavery; in many ways, they imagine them *for* the public. They imagine crime into existence in the social narrative—crime being a cultural construct (Davis 29) often associated with mad and disabled bodies (Cherney 19-20). It's easy for our social media feeds to disappear people into headlines, just like it's easy for prisons to disappear people (Davis 29). In so doing, importantly, mainstream media sets the terms of public discourse; media questions, asked supposedly on behalf of the public, model what terms people may engage in dialogue about a given topic. This proved true at the start of IMA during 2020, but it quickly proved true again as homelessness, as Qadhafi had predicted, become a hot topic in Kansas City media and public discourse. Although IMA's interventions were shaped by their specific position as a citizen journalism project, the broad strokes of their response—storytelling with epistemic justice, crip time, and power analysis—have potential application in community literacy work well beyond citizen journalism.

Media visibility around homelessness came at a cost for KCHU. News stations regularly walked into the KCHU occupation with cameras, invading people's privacy and homes and misconstruing the union's efforts. While mainstream coverage included KCHU for many months, the longer-lasting dialogue was around city initiatives and advocacy organizations; KCHU was made to fit into that dialogue, rather than leading it, despite city initiatives and advocacy groups being led entirely or almost entirely by people who had never experienced homelessness. IMA's primary intervention, at first, was an epistemic one; rather than forcing KCHU to fit a broader dialogue, IMA fit it to them. Throughout IMA's coverage, unhoused leaders were the first source, the ultimate authority on their own experiences. The first interview Qadhafi gave on behalf of the union was with Andrei, who ultimately ran a transcript of the entire interview with a brief introduction—something that was replicated in the numerous livestreams IMA did with KCHU members, a format which ensured people could and did speak for themselves.

IMA citizen journalists also regularly asked the union to verify what the city said about what kind of access they were creating for unhoused people–not the other way around. This flipped dominant narratives on their heads even as they were being written; while other outlets focused on city and nonprofit initiatives and sometimes wove the union into that, citizen journalists gave the same information but contextualized it through the lived experiences of unhoused activists. This continued into the next fall and winter, as the city's failure to plan for cold weather became quickly evident. IMA citizen journalists covered the city's failure, but especially as the year wore on, their questions highlighted unhoused-led solutions—people from the camp organizing mutual aid, creating jobs for homeless membership, and gathering and distributing supplies despite numerous setbacks, including theft of a large portion of early donations to KCHU.

Citizen journalism also proved more accommodating of the iterative, collective, and often messy portions of the union's various phases of work. IMA's position as a citizen journalism project meant they could, in a sense, work on and with crip time and its many facets (Samuels). Their journalists chose whom and what to cover, and coverage wasn't on their news deadline; it was something they could negotiate with the union and around their other work schedules. Among other upsides, this offered IMA the freedom and the flexibility to ensure its coverage centered on what unhoused leaders said—their solutions, their material needs, and their leadership. At the beginning of the occupation, this allowed IMA to take KCHU's demands into spaces of power—including, but not limited to, Andrei and I going after the mayor as he walked away from us, reading KCHU's demands back to him, and asking him to respond. We were there with cameras when he negotiated with Qadhafi for a hotel program that was supposed to be a precursor to permanent housing, and we were there when the union returned to city property when the city broke its promise.

On an immediate level, that kind of coverage—the consistent coverage of a few topics over a substantial period of time, which is common to citizen journalism (Greer and McLaughlin)—meant that when city officials tried to backtrack on promises, it wasn't activists' word against the city's; it was the city's claim against dozens of hours of live video proving them wrong. That is, citizen journalist coverage prevented those with material and discursive power from getting to frame the entire narrative. In storying KCHU's work, IMA's intervention wasn't just in creating documentation; it was an intervention in *access*—in ensuring the story of housing in Kansas City in 2021 didn't get to lose those bodies, and that the city's claim of creating "access" would either have to be access as defined by those most impacted, or else it would have to answer to an archive of stories about the embodied realities it overlooked.

Over the course of covering the union and other activist work in Kansas City, IMA has also built in practices to ensure its coverage of KCHU and other movements that attend to questions of power and amplify the most impacted–rather than just the loudest–voices as best we can. IMA has, for example, adapted feminist organizing tools like power analysis as a way of structuring both their questions on live interviews and their stories—something several citizen journalists and I gave a workshop on at the 2021 Conference on Community Writing. Organizers use power analysis to analyze formal (e.g., laws, policies, city government); hidden (e.g., lobbyists, economic interests, NGOs); and shadow (e.g., ideological, religious) power. However, IMA has taken the same analysis as a way of structuring stories that start with lived experience and then questions and exposes the power structures that impact it. In the process, citizen journalists often point their audience toward potential ways of intervening in and dismantling that power, such as when Andrei dug through files from the Fraternal Order of Police and drew attention to specific policies that enabled harm in Kansas City (Stoica, "The Blue Hand"). "Solutions-focused" journalism, for them, isn't focused on top-down solutions either—it's solutions like KCHU's, developed by and for those most impacted by a given problem. The way citizen journalists from IMA story movements for access, like KCHU's, makes intentional intervention into the gap between awareness and action that Nedra Reynolds identifies (20-26). This includes both asking questions that draw out grassroots solutions and using tools like social media to draw audiences into not just awareness, but involvement (see Stoica, "Introduction to Citizen Journalism" and Swank, "Using Social Media").

Conclusion

The KCHU camp was swept in February 2022, after a year of on and off occupation. The space where the occupation had moved in summer 2021—the lot at the corner of 10th and Harrison Street, just a few blocks from Kansas City, Missouri City Hall—has been turned into a dog park. It's not open, but, like city hall's front lawn, there's a fence around it now—public property barred from public access because the wrong public tried to access it. The union demanded a seat at the table and got a fence instead, and then another one, and now a dog park. However, in pushing for and modeling collective, self-determined access, KCHU not only exposed top-down city solutions as untenable; they also laid the groundwork for the relationships and movement that is them creating their own table, as multiple KCHU members have described since. Mutual aid work persists despite most of KCHU's funds for that work being stolen a few months ago. Qadhafi's LLC to employ homeless people continues, too, but quietly—for now.[4]

And here's where it matters to read this story as one that's about access–in the liberatory, crip sense of that word. Not all citizen journalism bothers to take up questions of access, who's responsible for creating it, what it really means, and whether it's liberatory or whether it simply replicates the same carceral social logics and institutionalized violences mainstream media so often does. But for IMA, storying activist work has looked like storying access with an abolitionist, liberatory access in mind. Their work demonstrates how community writing projects like theirs—whether they're citizen journalism or some other form of oral history or public storytelling—practice epistemic justice that has material impacts on public discourse. By framing their narratives around concepts that are echoed in disability justice like leadership of the most impacted, IMA could story housing in Kansas City in a way that got at collective, liberatory access rather than simply the top-down solutions that quickly came to dominate mainstream media discourse. Their intervention has looked like creating media narratives that try to help people see beyond prisons and policing as the solutions, and to recognize when what is actually being proposed as a solution is actually a prison, or police, and not life-affirming at all—and that extends well beyond coverage of stories like KCHU, even though how we frame and understand those stories shape how we understand and position access in the rest of our work.

For community writing work like IMA, stories create and are created by movements for access. Drawing out access as a theme has proven useful not just the actual writing and composing IMA does, but also for creating broader organizational practices, visions, and strategic plans. It's become a way of assessing impact, structuring conversations, and organizing citizen journalists to meet each other's needs so they can keep telling stories like KCHU's. That is, although IMA is not a disability justice organization per se, their work and the work of those whose stories they help tell is shaped deeply by questions of access—a small move, I think, toward creating the "autonomous, life-affirming community" Qadhafi talked about.

Notes

1. Often, terms like "unhoused" and "houseless" are preferred to "homeless" due to the stigma associated with "homeless" as well as, importantly, the implication that persons without permanent housing are without a "home"—something that often disguises the violence of something like a camp "sweep," where city officials (in most cities, Parks and Rec and/or police) destroying the encampments that unhoused individuals may in fact consider home. Many of the advocacy organizations (most of which are predominantly comprised of housed individuals) in Kansas City tend toward language like "unhoused" and "houseless" for this reason. However, the homeless activists I will be discussing in this section have explicitly told me they prefer—and intentionally use—the term "homeless," and see other terms as a way of trying to

soften the reality of homelessness through language. Out of respect for the complexity of the various perspectives on linguistic choices here, the importance of the homeless leaders whose work I discuss being allowed to self-define, and the recognition that there are differing viewpoints on these terms, I have made it a point to interchangeably use all these terms, preferring whenever possible the terms used by whomever I am describing at a given time.

2. All KCHU interviews are from 2021. Unlike other sources here, they are cited by date, because the timeline of KCHU's occupation, when in the year (seasons) they fall, and the duration for which they had these conversations and issued these demands are important context for the story. Only a small fraction of IMA's coverage of KCHU appears here. You can find the rest of the livestream and video coverage (including more than 15 extended interviews) at https://www.facebook.com/independentmediaus/. Articles are at https://www.independentmedia.us/.

3. Although the warming center was named "the Scott Eicke Warming Center," Sixx did not like or use his legal name, according to his ex-wife, so this article will not use it either (see Fitzsimmons, "In Memorium").

4. Both fundraising efforts and other mutual aid work are ongoing via KCHU's social media (https://www.facebook.com/kchomelessunion). Dialogue around housing also continues, with another KCHU leader, Davina Meyer, starting the Kansas City United Front Against Homelessness (https://www.facebook.com/groups/1104654573793545).

Livestreams

December 31, 2020. Stoica, Andrei. "Protest against houseless camp sweeps in KCMO." *Independent Media Association*. https://www.facebook.com/independentmediaus/videos/795175717730649

March 23, 2021. Fitzsimmons, Brynn. "Kansas City Homeless Union, occupation at KCMO City Hall." *Independent Media Association*. https://www.facebook.com/independentmediaus/videos/818201008907394

April 5, 2021. Fitzsimmons, Brynn. "Kansas City Homeless Union, City Hall, Kansas City," Missouri. *Independent Media Association*. https://www.facebook.com/independentmediaus/videos/4585057891527954

September 22, 2021. Stoica, Andrei. "Kansas City Homeless Union Update." Kansas City, Missouri. *Independent Media Association*. https://www.facebook.com/independentmediaus/videos/4585057891527954

Works Cited

Allan, Stuart. *Citizen Witnessing: Revisioning Journalism in Times of Crisis*. John Wiley & Sons, 2013.

Allan, Stuart, and Esther Thorson. *Citizen Journalism: Global Perspectives*. Peter Lang, 2009.

Bailey, Moya. "Misogynoir in Medical Media: On Caster Semenya and R. Kelly." *Catalyst: Feminism, Theory, Technoscience*, vol. 2, no. 2, 2, Sept. 2016, pp. 1–31, https://doi.org/10.28968/cftt.v2i2.28800.

Bailey, Moya, and Whitney Peoples. "Articulating Black Feminist Health Science Studies." *Catalyst: Feminism, Theory, Technoscience*, vol. 3, no. 2, 2017, https://doi.org/10.28968/cftt.v3i2.28844.

Ben-Moshe, Liat. *Decarcerating Disability: Deinstitutionalization and Prison Abolition*. University of Minnesota Press, 2020.

Borda, Jennifer L., and Bailey Marshall. "Creating a Space to #SayHerName: Rhetorical Stratification in the Networked Sphere." *Quarterly Journal of Speech*, vol. 106, no. 2, Apr. 2020, pp. 133–55. https://doi.org/10.1080/00335630.2020.1744182.

Cedillo, Christina V. "What Does It Mean to Move?: Race, Disability, and Critical Embodiment Pedagogy." *Composition Forum*, vol. 39, Summer 2018, https://compositionforum.com/issue/39/to-move.php.

Cherney, James L. *Ableist Rhetoric: How We Know, Value, and See Disability*. Penn State Press, 2019.

Davis, Angela Y. *Abolition Democracy: Beyond Empire, Prisons, and Torture*. Seven Stories Press, 2011.

Davis, Angela Y., Gina Dent, Erica R. Meiners, Beth E. Ritchie. *Abolition. Feminism. Now*. Haymarket Books, 2022.

Fitzsimmons, Brynn. "In Memoriam: Scott 'Sixx' Eicke." *Independent Media Association*, 23 Jan. 2021, https://www.independentmedia.us/home/media-archive/january-2021/in-memoriam-scott-sixx-eicke.

Greer, Chris, and Eugene McLaughlin. "We Predict a Riot?: Public Order Policing, New Media Environments and the Rise of the Citizen Journalist." *The British Journal of Criminology*, vol. 50, no. 6, 2010, pp. 1041–59.

Jackson, Cody A., and Christina V. Cedillo. "We Are Here to Crip That Shit: Embodying Accountability beyond the 'Word.'" *College Composition and Communication*, vol. 72, no. 1, 2020, pp. 109–17.

Kafer, Alison. *Feminist, Queer, Crip*. Indiana University Press, 2013.

Mingus, Mia. "Beyond Access: Mia Mingus on Disability Justice." *EquitableEducation.Ca*, 30 Nov. 2013, https://EquitableEducation.ca/2013/mia-mingus-disability-justice.

Noterman, Elsa, and Eli Meyerhoff. "Revolutionary Scholarship by Any Speed Necessary: Slow or Fast but for the End of This World." *ACME: An International Journal for Critical Geographies*, Jan. 2017.

paperson, la. *A Third University Is Possible*. U of Minnesota Press, 2017.

Piepzna-Samarasinha, Leah Lakshmi. *Care Work: Dreaming Disability Justice*. Arsenal Pulp Press, 2018.

Price, Margaret. *Mad at School: Rhetorics of Mental Disability and Academic Life*. University of Michigan Press, 2011.

Puar, Jasbir K. *The Right to Maim: Debility, Capacity, Disability*. Duke University Press Books, 2017.

Reynolds, Nedra. *Geographies of Writing: Inhabiting Places and Encountering Difference*. Southern Illinois University Press, 2003.

Rodríguez, Dylan. "Racial/Colonial Genocide and the 'Neoliberal Academy': In Excess of a Problematic." *American Quarterly*, vol. 64, no. 4, 2012, pp. 809–13.

Samuels, Ellen. "Six Ways of Looking at Crip Time." *Disability Studies Quarterly*, vol. 37, no. 3, 3, Aug. 2017.

Schalk, Sami. *Bodyminds Reimagined: (Dis)Ability, Race, and Gender in Black Women's Speculative Fiction*. Duke University Press, 2018.

Schenwar, Maya, et al. *Prison by Any Other Name: The Harmful Consequences of Popular Reforms*. The New Press, 2020.

Sins Invalid. "10 Principles of Disability Justice." *Sins Invalid: An Unshamed Claim to Beauty in the Face of Invisibility*, 17 Sept. 2015, https://www.sinsinvalid.org/blog/10-principles-of-disability-justice.

Stanley, Eric A. "Gender Self-Determination." *TSQ: Transgender Studies Quarterly*, vol. 1, no. 1–2, May 2014, pp. 89–91, https://doi.org/10.1215/23289252-2399695.

Stanley, Eric A., and Nat Smith. *Captive Genders: Trans Embodiment and the Prison Industrial Complex*. AK Press, 2015.

Stoica, Andrei. "The Fraternal Order of Police: The Blue Hand Around the Throat of Kansas City, Missouri" *Independent Media Association*, editorial, 10 October 2020, https://www.independentmedia.us/home/editorials/the-fraternal-order-of-police-the-blue-hand-around-the-throat-of-kcmo.

—. "'My Current Address Is 414 East 12th Street, City Hall, Homeless at Large': Organizer Speaks on Homeless Union." *Independent Media Association*, 5 Feb. 2021, https://www.independentmedia.us/home/media-archive/february-2021/my-current-address-is-414-east-12th-street-city-hall.

—. "Introduction to Citizen Journalism," in *Citizen Journalism 101, Independent Media Association*, https://www.independentmedia.us/education/citizen-journalism-101-training-series/introduction-to-citizen-journalism.

Swank, Bekah. "Using Social Media to Deepen Engagement with the News," in *Citizen Journalism 101, Independent Media Association*, https://www.independentmedia.us/education/citizen-journalism-101-training-series/using-social-media-to-deepen-engagement-with-the-news.

Taylor, Sonya Renee. *The Body Is Not an Apology: The Power of Radical Self-Love*. Berrett-Koehler Publishers, 2018.

Author Bio

Brynn Fitzsimmons is a PhD candidate in English – Rhetoric and Composition (certificate in Women's, Gender, and Sexuality Studies) at the University of Kansas. Their current research focuses on rhetorics of bodies, health, and access at the intersections of abolitionist activist movements, public and community writing, disability studies, and feminist and queer cultural rhetorics. They have a book chapter on representations of mental and chronic illness in Netflix's *Afflicted* that recently appeared in *Streaming Mental Health and Illness: Essays on Representation in Netflix Original Programs*, edited by Emily Katseanes. They are an associate editor for Kansas City-based citizen journalism project *Independent Media Association*, a contributing writer for the blog of *Synapsis: A Health Humanities Journal*, and a blog editor for Liberation Lit, which sends books and letters to people incarcerated in Kansas and Missouri.

Everything You Need to Eat: Food, Access, and Community

Tyler Martinez

Abstract

Skills, knowledge, time, ability, access, and cultural and societal norms all sponsor and constrain food literacies. Measuring the effects of class, race, cultural identity, knowledge, and ability on food access requires an understanding of how communities and institutions sponsor food literacy. Nutritionists have developed a framework for researching and measuring food literacy; however, the focus falls on measuring individual food literacy, which I argue is a form of *epistemic whiteness* that refuses to acknowledge the outsized responsibility of institutions in creating systems of food access and flattens the role community plays in mitigating barriers to access. A critical understanding of disability and the reciprocity intrinsic to community literacy research are offered as a way to move from measurement to sponsorship of community food literacies.

Keywords

food literacy, food access, disability studies, community literacy, sustainability

I left catfish and white bean Fridays when I moved to Virginia, those evenings when my innumerous extended family crowded around my grandparents' too-small kitchen. I left those *ça fait chaud* afternoons fishing off the deck behind my aunt's house with my cousins. I can't follow my dad around the competitive jambalaya circuit or drive my mom and I to New Orleans for a food fest on the riverfront. I don't get to spend my evenings in the kitchen with my sister, benefiting from the knowledge she earned over the course of a four-year culinary degree. I don't have immediate access to the friends that I gathered over a decade of slinging lattes and building sandwiches across South Louisiana.

I struggled to understand and access the habits of food that would sustain me when I started a Ph.D. program. I landed in a glorified doctoral dorm negotiating for access to fridge space and microwave minutes, navigating frozen-burrito and fast-foodways that are expensive and difficult to access. When seminars let out at 10pm, I headed to the grocery store to forage–determined to buy something to eat but not knowing quite what to expect to find that I'd be willing and able to eat. A thousand miles from the Cajun and Creole foodways that sustained my 29 years, I was lonely and hungry and unsure of how to eat sustainably on a graduate student's salary in one of the largest metro areas in the world. And too often, my anxieties about being the *best student* and the cyclical depressive crash still cause me to neglect even attempting to access food.

There's a different story to tell about why I chose to leave Louisiana to pursue a Ph.D. and academic career, but queer-trauma fueled anxiety and depression kept me from feeling like I had any opportunity to succeed there. I could always count on community to provide another meal, whether it was my mom coming through with gumbo she purposefully made too much of or a friend inviting me to a "staff" party at a restaurant in the French Quarter. I expected to struggle to advance an academic career because I was literally raised in a swamp, but I didn't expect that the combination of my mental disability and a shock of *habitus* would so disrupt my ability to access food. The foodways that we inhabit are more complex than habit would have us realize.

When it comes to food, access is survival. Access to food requires community–a community that respects the needs of its members even when it can't fully understand them. From an intuitive interdisciplinary definition, nutrition scientists have developed food literacy into a set of domains and components. Those domains and components construct an ontology and methodology useful for quantifying food literacy to facilitate its measurement. The primary domain of food literacy is access, specifically, "being able to access food through some source on a regular basis with very limited resources," is highlighted by experts as the core component of food literacy. Pierre Bourdieu's concept of *habitus* is useful for visualizing the networks that connect individuals and communities to food within social and political institutions (Power 48). Individual's *habitus* of food–the confluence of skill, knowledge, experience, ability, and ideology–sponsors practices of access. I borrow that sense of "sponsorship" from Deborah Brandt's work; literacies are enabled or constrained through the sponsorship of individuals, communities, and institutions. The constraints of food access on a community are determined by global food systems that are prone to sudden disruption–disrupting access disrupts survival.

I started researching food literacy because I struggled to find the time and energy to access enough food. And I wasn't quiet or passive about it. I touched every level of bureaucracy trying to figure out how to navigate food and access to kitchen equipment in Northern Virginia. First, I researched SNAP benefits, but the stipend associated with my fellowship provides just enough that I don't qualify, being single with no dependents, for the program. The campus community pantry left a bag with my name in the student union, filled with uncooked pasta and a couple cans of high-fructose corn syrup laden sauce–nothing I had the equipment to prepare. A financial advisor/administrator suggested I take out more loans. In my research, I met a professor in the nutrition department–she introduced me to the graduate student who manages the campus gardens and food forest. I learned a lot about the culture surrounding food on campus and in Northern Virginia, like the fact that Fairfax County operates a Food Access and Literacy Work Group which influences the food system I was learning to navigate. My emails to the director of that group went unanswered. No one had any actionable advice that could help me circumvent the habits that seemed my only option. I was looking in the wrong places for the community food access that is baked into Cajun and Creole cultures.

As a framework, the domains and components of food literacy are valuable to scholars who, like me, study at the intersections of literacy and food access. They provide an extensive vocabulary with which to discuss the complexity of foodways—the social and political networks which sponsor food access. Food access is constrained by class, gender, ability, and race; however, research into food access in the field of food literacy is largely uncritical of definitions of disability and relies on preconceived barriers to access (Schwartz et al. 107). Specifically surrounding the concept of "individuals" and "communities," the field of food literacy could work to further remove the tinge of essentialism derived from the parent discipline, nutrition. *Food Literacy* essentializes the *habitus* of experience that affects minoritized racial and cultural groups and obfuscates the barriers to access for people with disabilities. The false binary between individuals' food choices as primarily nutritional or social fails to account for the complexities of how institutions sponsor food literacy.

There is a long history of food access discrimination against people of color and people with disabilities, such as anti-foraging laws and corporate discrimination.

> Eight percent of black Americans live in a census tract with a supermarket, compared to 31% of white Americans. Nationally, low-income zip codes have 30% more convenience stores–which are less likely than supermarkets to stock healthy foods–than middle-income zip codes. Ultimately, low-income communities lack viable access to healthy foods and are therefore forced to turn to unhealthy foods that are within their physical and economic reach (DePasquale et al. 912-913).

Those foodways forced on low-income Americans are unsustainable and corporatist– but teaching low-income students that the only foodways to which they have access are unsustainable without also sponsoring community literacies (and/or institutions) of food that are more sustainable *for them* potentially creates another barrier to access by adding anxiety to food insecurity.

By framing food access as the responsibility of the individual, *Food Literacy* works from what Dr. Kimberlé Crenshaw terms *epistemic whiteness*. Epistemic whiteness is a refusal "to assess and transform relationships of domination and equality across the social field," (13). Individualism in food access upholds epistemic whiteness by reifying the illusion that individuals have power over systems of food access. The communities of food *habitus* that I've found sustaining aren't accounted for in food literacy's framework, so I posit instead an intersectional, interdisciplinary community food literacy that can research, measure, *and* sponsor accessible and sustainable foodways for everyone.

Helen Vigden, author of *Food Literacy,* and her colleagues call for international consensus on a definition of food literacy, citing fifty-one different definitions in use in 2019 (Thompson et al. 1). As nutrition scientists argue, defining food literacy is important for the project of measuring food literacy. But progress can be made before and beyond an international governmental agency decides to take up any one definition of food literacy with intersectional, interdisciplinary attention to communities' *habitus* of food. And those of us in literacy studies are primed to offer a transformational perspective. We take as the focus of our research and pedagogy the sponsorship of literacies rather than the measurement of literacies. Dr. Veronica House (2014) describes the benefits of food literacy-focused service-learning curriculum in writing courses, to sponsor written literacies and broaden their food literacies. To this intersection I add the perspective of an anxious, queer Cajun, as an expansion of the possibilities of food literacy in the writing classroom and a call for literacy scholars to engage in the burgeoning field of food literacy.

Food literacy, as I understand it, is scaffolded with access at the base. The domains of food literacy, as identified through Vigden's collaborative research, are access, planning and management, selection, knowing where food comes from, preparation, eating, nutrition, and language (Vigden 37-48). Access is the foundation on which the other domains build. The components of food access developed by nutrition scientists are:

1.1 Being able to find food anywhere, that you can eat.

1.2 Being able to access food through some source on a regular basis with very limited resources.

1.3 Knowing that some places are cheaper than others.

1.4 Knowing how to access the shop, how to access the funds to purchase what you require and the knowledge in regard to if it's not coming from a shop for example, bush foods, aid agencies.

1.5 Getting out in the garden and growing food, even if it's herbs in a pot.

1.6 Being critical of the food supply system and being able to advocate for improvements. (Vigden 37)

These components of food access flatten the embodied experience of accessing food as an individual, subjected to the constraints of global foodways. Components 1.1, 1.3, and 1.4 are ranked as "desirable" for food access. Component 1.3 is the "core" component, and components 1.5 and 1.6 were ranked as "irrelevant." Component 1.1 centralizes the needs of the individual; however, the application of that component to the community or nation creates room for the voice of people with disabilities to be overlooked. When applied to the nation, who is the "you" in finding food anywhere that you can eat? Is it the person with the least access or a consensus–the average of food access enjoyed by the majority? Each component requires certain skills and knowledge, but 1.4 is of particular interest; it situates the individual in a network of economies, environments, and social programs, that combine to produce food systems.

Vigden asserts that food literacy applies at the "individual, household, community, and national levels to protect diet quality through change and support dietary resilience over time" (151). Food access applies at the level of the individual and household because they must use the other domains–language, preparation, selection, eating, etc.–to materialize their access to food. It is the responsibility of communities and especially states and nations to build food systems that supply regular access to individuals and households. Individuals and even households cannot legally produce everything they need to eat in contemporary foodways–they produce resources to exchange for what they need, but with rare exception households in capitalist nations are not growing, hunting, or foraging for everything that they need to eat—and usually not even a portion of it.

A scoping review by Schwartz et al. highlights the gaps in research that projects measuring food literacy could seek to fill. The research team compiled 106 qualitative and quantitative articles, thirty-two of which focused on the association between disability and household food insecurity (HFI). "Disability was consistently related to an increase in HFI" and access to household assets is more protective for people with disabilities than increased income (Schwartz et al. 112). Even so, "Research from the United States suggests that people with disability may require an income two to three-times greater to avoid HFI due to added medical and adaptive equipment expenses, costs for personal assistants, or special dietary needs" (Schwartz et al. 112). At the level of the individual, people with disabilities need more income for food access because they must navigate social systems of access that are more costly for non-normative bodies.

Social networks can "mediate the relationship between disability and food" depending on the social environment (Schwartz et al. 112). At the community level, the food literacy of the group compensates for barriers to access faced by individuals; "qualitative research indicates that adequate social supports were able to compensate for inadequate geographical access or poor economic access…" (Schwartz et al. 112). Social networks can become barriers to food access as "social norms and values influence food access patterns" (Schwartz et al. 112). The social programs that provide food access to people living with food insecurity are often stigmatized which influence individuals' experiences of community food literacy.

Beyond social networks, institutional and organizational policies are a primary determiner of food access.

> Access to social benefits varied across studies populations. Access to disability benefits could be limited by bureaucratic systems and requirements to prove disability. People who fail to qualify because they are "not disabled enough" or fail to fit within includable types of disability are particularly disadvantaged. (Schwartz et al. 113)

I argue that food literacy applies at the level of the institution or nation first because institutional policies create persistent barriers to access for individuals with disabilities. Measuring individual food literacy requires assessing an individual's ability to navigate social programs and institutions, as indicated by component 1.4. Those of us interested in researching at the intersections of food access, literacy, and disability must "better consider the experiences of people with disabilities, rather than preconceiving disabling barriers" (Schwartz et al. 115). This includes the students in our classes that are relying on resources like campus pantries to have enough to eat.

Food literacy, as a framework, is criticized for being "over theorized and under practiced" as many are (Renwick and Smith 18). The limitations of the application of food literacy have resulted in a field of scholarship that focuses on the individual rather than communities or institutions and places "an overwhelming emphasis on food, with far less attention being paid to literacy" (Renwick and Smith 18). To combat the epistemic whiteness implicit in the focus on measuring individual food literacy, the methodologies that circulate in community literacy help to foreground reciprocal research. Food literacy research is always community literacy research because food literacy is always a community literacy. In a previous special issue of this journal Dawn S. Opel and Donnie Johnson Sackey cite two decades of research that asserts "Reciprocity as a Guiding Principle for Community-Engaged Research" which "asks us to establish networks of reciprocity via a self-reflexive rhetoric that includes:"

1. a reconsideration of how we define and categorize oppression before we enter communities;

2. a recognition of how we gain access to the lives of people outside universities;

3. a commitment to reciprocity, which necessitates the involvement of community partners in the interpretation of data and in how we tell stories that are not our own;

4. and an emphasis on scholarly activism, or commitment to effectuating change (1).

Scholars in literacy, rhetoric, and writing studies offer reciprocity as a self-reflexive framework for measuring food literacy that both centers community agency and works from a critical understanding of literacy.

In accordance with the *Ten Principles of Disability Justice* as articulated by Patty Berne and Sins Invalid, collective access to food fosters *collective liberation* as the struggle for survival costs less time, labor, and emotional resources for everyone. Progress in the field of food literacy will happen when the framework is influenced by research *lead by those most impacted*, such as people with disabilities and other minoritized communities. Schwartz et al. illustrate the current pressing need for more research at the intersections of food access, household food insecurity (HFI), and disability; just eight of the 106 articles in their scoping review started with a critical definition of disability. "A social model of disability can inform future research by acknowledging the role of socio-environmental influences on the production and experience(s) of disability" (Schwartz et al. 107). Food systems should be *sustainable* and food literacy requires *interdependence*. The *habitus* of food that the field of food literacy ultimately reifies or creates should be built from the principle of *collective access*; collective access requires consulting individuals and communities who live with minoritized ability, race, gender, or class identities when developing food literacy frameworks. Access to food is survival and building food systems that foster collective access to food is love.

Research at the intersections of disability and food access should, as Schwartz et al. posit, interact critically with the definition of disability, reconsidering how researchers define and categorize oppression before studying communities of disabled people and people with disabilities. From the outside, my food insecurity might look like laziness or antisocial behavior, but my mental disability and cultural background create barriers to food access that are difficult to discern from the outside. In that way, reciprocity *recognizes the wholeness* and value of the embodied experience of research subjects. Reciprocity as a guiding principle also encourages *leadership of the most impacted* in the interpretation of data.

The emphasis that a reciprocal framework places on "scholarly activism, or commitment to effectuating change" and the "anti-capitalist politic" of the *Ten Principles of Disability Justice* combine to produce non-conforming bodies advocating to disrupt the profitability of food systems in order to foster equitable access. And we must recognize that capitalist food systems are unsustainable–a food literacy framework should foster sustainable habits of food from the individual to the global level. Researchers must "pace ourselves, individually and collectively, to be sustained long term. Our embodied experiences guide us toward ongoing justice and liberation" (Sins Invalid). Individual *habitus* is not to be blamed for institutional foodways; however, whenever possible we must all look critically at the sustainability of our *habitus* of food to start to foster *collective access*.

I haven't had the space or resources yet to imagine what it might look like to sponsor food literacy for my students in Writing and Rhetoric. As I write this, I haven't had students in Virginia, and it will likely be years before I have the opportunity to spend time on a community-engaged project that might sponsor food literacy for my students and their communities simultaneously while also making those foodways accessible for research. Until I can convince someone to allow me that space, I've found a comfortable level of existence and can offer my experiences and some theory. I also hope that others might take up the call.

I used the idle time between bites on the fishing line to make lists of all the adjectives I'd one day use to describe the fertility of the swamps, to persuade the rest of the world to respect them the way my community does. The community in "cancer alley"–that stretch of Highway 90 between New Orleans and Baton Rouge affectionately named for the oil refineries that pollute the land and water–works the land to keep its people from going hungry. But it is succumbing ever more rapidly to climate change caused by neoliberal capitalist consumption that includes, in no small part, individualist foodways.

Community is a privilege in this age of hyper-individualistic social disaggregation, but community is a necessity for sustainable foodways, especially for those of us with intersectionally minoritized identity categories. I had a hard time thinking of myself as food insecure, even when surviving on a single daily on-campus meal and enjoying almost nothing I ate. When I requested assistance from the university, I was forced to sign a form attesting that I was food insecure. The stigma associated with social services was overwhelming; I almost didn't check the box. I was eating, after all. A friend had to remind me that, yes, I was experiencing food insecurity; "you mostly come here to use our kitchen." I turned my friends' kitchens into safe spaces of Cajun food *habitus* where I could relax and prepare inexpensive, nutritious food for myself and my queer chosen family. For all my research in food literacy and all the administrators I bothered, it was queer community that helped me to access food in ways that are comforting and sustaining rather than fraught.

Let's infuse that vibe into our research and teaching focused on food access and food literacy. As literacy scholars, we can bring the nuance of community literacy sponsorship to other disciplines while allowing food literacy to infiltrate how we discuss food and foodways in our disciplines. The barriers to food access posed by my mental disability and cultural background–my *habitus* of food–were mitigated in part through queer community building. The epistemic whiteness that places responsibility for food access on the individual also creates inaccessible institutions like my campus's student pantry. Communities of food access are necessary for all of us, so it is in everyone's best interest to sponsor sustainable community food literacies.

Works Cited

Brandt, Deborah. "Sponsors of Literacy." *College Composition and Communication*, vol. 42, no. 4, 1998, 165–185. JSTOR. https://doi.org/10.2307/358929

Crenshaw, Kimberlé Williams. "Introduction." *Seeing Race Again: Countering Colorblindness Across the Disciplines*. Okaland, California: University of California Press, 2019. Print. pp. 1-19.

De Pasquale, Dan, Surbhi Sarang, and Natalie Bump Vena. "Forging Food Justice Through Cooperatives in New York." *Fordham Urban Law Journal*, vol. 45, no. 4, 2018. Print. pp. 909-949.

House, Veronica. "Re-Framing the Argument: Critical Service-Learning and Community-Centered Food Literacy." *Community Literacy Journal*, vol. 8, no. 2, 2014, pp. 1-16. DOI:10.25148/clj.8.2.009307.

Opel, Dawn S, and Donnie Johnson Sackey. "Reciprocity in Community-Engaged Food and Environmental Justice Scholarship." *Community Literacy Journal*, vol. 14, no. 1, 2019. pp. 1-6. DOI: https://doi.org/10.1353/clj.2019.0027.

Power, Elaine M. "An Introduction to Pierre Bourdieu's Key Theoretical Concepts." *Journal for the Study of Food and Society*, 3:1, 1999. p. 48-52. DOI: https://doi.org/10.2752/152897999786690753.

Ten Principles of Disability Justice, created Patty Berne and Sins Invalid. https://www.sinsinvalid.org/blog/10-principles-of-disability-justice. Accessed 10 March 2022.

Thompson, Courtney, Jean Adams and Helen Anna Vidgen. "Are we Closer to International Consensus on the Term 'Food Literacy'? A Systematic Scoping Review of Its Use in the Academic Literature (1998-2019)." *Nutrients*, 13, 2021, p. 1-24. DOI: https://doi.org/10.3390/nu13062006.

Renwick, Kerry and Mary Gale Smith. "The Political Action of Food Literacy: A Scoping Review." *Journal of Family and Consumer Sciences*, 112:1, 2020. p. 14-22. DOI: 10.14307/JFCS112.1.14.

Schwartz, Naomi, Ron Buliung, and Kathi Wilson. "Disability and food access and insecurity: A scoping review of the literature." *Health & Place,* 57, 2019. p. 107-121. DOI: https://doi.org/10.1016/j.healthplace.2019.03.011.

Vigden, Helen. *Food Literacy: Key Concepts for Health and Education.* Routledge, New York, NY, 2016. Print.

Author Bio

Tyler Martinez is an intellectual po'boy – a queer, Cajun, first-generation Ph.D. student of Writing and Rhetoric at George Mason University in Virginia. He earned both a B.A. in Linguistics and an M.A. in Rhetoric and Composition at the University of Louisiana at Lafayette. Before becoming a full-time purveyor of language, he worked for a decade as a barista, server, and line cook in restaurants across South Louisiana. He hopes to continue to explore the intersections of queerness, disability studies, community literacy, and food access.

Rethinking Access: Recognizing Privileges and Positionalities in Building Community Literacy

Sweta Baniya

Abstract

> This article rethinks digital access and community literacy by sharing aspects of intentional engagement informed by social justice frameworks to establish community partnerships that empower communities both local and global with digital literacy. The article explores access, privileges, and positionalities that the author strategically utilizes to support the communities within her current locality and in her hometown Nepal. By showcasing multiple intentional and equitable partnerships informed via social justice frameworks, the article argues that we require a transnational context to redefine digital literacy and our students need to understand these contexts better given the demands of the current workplace.

Keywords

> digital literacy, access, social justice, equitable engagement, international partnerships

Introduction

> Story 1: "I spent my lifetime in the kitchen…and educating me was never a priority for my family" said Him Kumari Baniya ("Midlife Education")

My 70-year-old *fupu* (aunt) said the above in an interview she gave in 2013 when she was taking a *Praud Sikhsya* (adult literacy) class that I enrolled her into. Although my *fupu* only has one eye, she still eagerly pursued her studies until COVID-19 hit. When I moved to the U.S., my *fupu* needed access to a smart phone to call me daily, which meant that she needed to become digitally literate. On good Internet days and when she can find my image on Viber, a phone application, my *fupu* and I engage in fruitful chats. That's our daily routine.

> Story 2: Even before COVID, the Code for Nepal team saw firsthand how teachers in public schools in remote parts of Nepal struggled with digital literacy. Some people, for example, owned laptops but did not know how to use them. (CEO of Code for Nepal)

Ravi Kumar, the CEO of Code for Nepal, has been working since 2014 to enhance digital literacy in remote locations throughout Nepal. As Ravi shared in my class in a lecture, people might have access to computers, but they do not know how to use them, a fact that shocked the students of my Fall 2020 Creating User Documentation course in the professional and technical writing program at Virginia Tech University who belonged to majorly belonged to computer science and writing majors. On the brighter side, UNSECO reports that the literacy rate of adult females in Nepal has risen from 9.153% in 1981 to 59.724% in 2018, which is a significant jump. This shows that things are changing. Even though literacy is on rise, the digital literacy required to keep up with this century's endless technological advancements is still at 31%, which is a notably low rate (Sen).

> *Story 3: Basic digital literacy is a necessity in our workplace as many of the resources available to employees are in a digital environment. Our Dining Hall Staff cannot access basic things like emails, W-2s, and the employee portal. (Linda Eaton & Kathrine Radford, Student Affairs, Virginia Tech University)*

When Linda Eaton & Kathrine Radford from Student Affairs at Virginia Tech University shared this with my Fall 2021 Creating User Documentation course in the professional and technical writing program, the students were surprised to learn that some people in our community and within our own university do not know how to use their phones or perform daily tasks on digital platforms that are necessary for survival in the United States. A lot of the dining hall and housekeeping staff members who are on daily wages come from lower economic backgrounds within our community or they are immigrants or refugees who are unfamiliar with the English language and most of them have never gone to school. Even though they work and live in a highly advanced and digital space among the tech-savvy students, the community members encounter all sorts of obstacles while living their day to day lives in our communities, one of which includes the hurdle of digital literacy.

In the stories I shared above, five concepts intersect: a) gender, b) privilege, c) access, d) education, and e) digital literacy. All these conceptual intersections are present pedagogically in my classes where students aim to understand these challenges and work towards contributing to the communities near and far to them. In this article, I describe partnerships that I have forged with two different local and global communities. By showcasing intentional and equitable engagement practices informed by social justice framework, I argue that scholars invested in community building can contribute to the global community by rethinking access, by recognizing their own privileges and positionalities, and by challenging the factors that impede access to different forms of literacies in the community we live and work in (Cushman; Mathieu). Such equity-oriented work could focus on establishing partnerships within our localities and across borders.

Literacy has always been challenged and is easily accessible to a certain class, gender and not accessible to some members. Literacy is also challenged by compounding crises, patriarchal norms, access to education, and how complexities and power imbalances create a lack of access and equity. Community engaged scholars in the field of rhetoric, writing, and technical communication have tried to tactically address these challenges by forging partnerships with community-driven organizations and by making written contributions (Hubrig; Mathieu; Parks; Shah). Such partnerships, which Steve Parks describes as "connecting its [partnerships] practices to underrepresented populations via service-learning projects," are not new in the field of rhetoric, writing, and technical communication (508). Community engaged scholars in the past few decades have been investing their research and teaching time in service-learning work. As argued by Veronica House, "when practitioners tie rhetoric and composition learning objectives to community initiatives that promote social justice, students' community-based work can offer powerful, active-learning experiences" (12). Such active-learning experiences lead both the community and the students towards a common goal, resulting in an awareness of social justice, privilege, power, and access issues. While active-learning experiences can have helpful outcomes, we must also acknowledge the concerns that emerge when integrating an active-learning course in a university curriculum. Some scholars, for example, worry that service learning only works to promote the university agenda; others share concern that the charity model of service learning reinforces stereotypes and some corporatized and militarized (Stoecker and Tryon 3; Kannan et al. 77). Such dissatisfactory university work and agendas can be and should be challenged with "contemplative work," which Paula Mathieu defines as antiracist work that puts people together in a variety of practices and can lead to a "realization [that] can support more empathy and compassion" (46). This also requires putting community needs first as well as working together with them to support them without any agenda of gain from that experience. Hence, in this article I rethink digital access and community literacy by sharing aspects of intentional engagement informed by social justice framework to establish community partnerships that empower communities with digital literacy. I explore the access, privileges, and positionalities that I strategically utilize to support the communities within my current locality and in my hometown Nepal. Finally, I argue that we require a transnational context to redefine digital literacy and our students need to understand these contexts better given the demands of current workplace.

Access & Digital Literacy

Issues of access have been a prominent concern for community engaged scholars and practitioners who continue to support the communities who have such needs. Scholars have been engaged in the issues of food literacy (House), second language learning (Swacha), community publishing (Parks), housing (Mathieu and George), adult and young children's literacy (Kumari), refugee integration (Powell), and technology literacy (Selfe). Most recently, Ada Hubrig has argued for disability justice which demands access and makes a critical point that access issues are more than simply disability (148). Access should be understood from a multidimensional perspective and intersections of gender, able bodies, privileges, and location to name a few. The above examples showcase that gender becomes a barrier to literacy. While owning a laptop or a smart digital phone can be a privilege, not knowing how to turn it on creates another barrier, even when one is educated. And, in the context of highly advanced university people's lives have been hindered due to lack of digital literacy. Then a question arises, how do we assess who is successful because of literacy or access? Cynthia

Selfe notes that "the definition of literacy determines not only who will succeed in our culture – and the criteria for such success –but also who will fail" (18). While Selfe articulated this in the context of the U.S., this argument seems contextual to other places where literacy and access to literacy hinders one's personal success. Those who have access have power.

Marginalization and a lack of access to education, food, and digital tools are interrelated and provide a circular argument where marginalization creates a lack of access, and a lack of access marginalizes people. Alondra Kiawitl Espejel et al. share that, "despite this highly successful intervention for amending institutional neglect, the ongoing lack of access and educational inequity at all levels remain fundamental challenges for the Chicano-Latino community in the twenty-first century" (33). Such challenges that stem from a lack of access continue to prevent the success of the marginalized community and their literacy, further deepening the unequal circumstances. Hubrig argues that "crafting spaces that don't consider the experience of people of color, of women, of poor, LGBTQA, and other body minds considered non-normative is also an issue of access" (148). When the needs of marginalized people are not taken into consideration by the people in power who can make changes, the issue of access arises that needs to be tackled with "strategies [that] demolish the systems which create barriers" (Hubrig 148). In current digital world marginalization happens via multiple contexts and a lack of access and barriers such as language and literacy. Further, a lack of digital literacy significantly hinders one's capacities of navigating the digital world.

Shifting towards the current world's situation affected by the COVID-19 pandemic and the digital divide, the Black, Indigenous, and people of color (BIPOC), including immigrants and refugees, are left behind due to a lack of access to digital tools, the Internet, and/or digital literacy (Beaunoyer et al.). Such marginalization due to a lack of digital literacy has happened across the world, including in advanced countries such as the United States. The issue of technological literacy was raised in the field by Selfe two decades ago. She states that technology literacy is beyond the basic functional understanding of computers and how they work but "rather, technological literacy refers to a complex set of socially and culturally situated values, practices, and skills involved in operating linguistically within the context of electronic environments, including reading, writing, and communicating" (11). Such literacies support people to navigate various technological apparatuses including the current digital environments. Technology literacy in current world could also be considered as digital literacy while they may not be synonymous. At its simplest definition, digital literacy is "a set of knowledge, skills, and attitudes that empower learners to engage with their digital lives" (Digital Literacy Framework). Teresa M. Dobson and John Willinksy argue that "the digital aspect of literacy, invisible to the naked eye, is the very currency that drives the global information economy" (286). The digital world requires people to have certain forms of digital literacy in order to be able to consume information, to write, and to be a part of the information economy. Sharma et al. point out that while globalization and technological developments have opened more pathways for digital information flows, knowledge as a competitive asset may not have reached their rightful beneficiaries (628). Access to digital literacy is often hindered by educational literacy, financial ability to purchase digital tools, or Internet access. Moreover, the accessibility and design of digital tools can also lead to lack of digital literacy.

A study conducted by the U.S. Department of Education on Digital literacy estimates that 31.8 million Americans do not have sufficient competence with digital technologies, especially computers. Those who are not digitally literate are most likely to be Black, Hispanic, or foreign-born (Kavensky). While unequal circumstances persist and worsen due to the COVID-19 pandemic, a culture of global community care and equity should be established by rethinking what it means to have access. The digitally literate population was able to adjust and adapt to the digital challenges brought on by the pandemic, however, many were left behind. The global pandemic has shown us that access is determined by privileges and positionalities because the most vulnerable in the world continue to suffer from a lack of access to necessities such as vaccines. This form of injustice, vaccine inequity, and the continuing struggle of underserved and marginalized communities across the globe should be discussed in classrooms and other spaces. Hence, it is prime time for community engaged scholars to rethink access by exploring the exclusionary practices and systems of oppression (Collins; Crenshaw) that make someone visible and invisible (Cedillo) and determine what one can and cannot access.

We need to think of access and digital literacy through a critical lens because digital literacy is an issue of equity and justice. The Digital Literacy Framework created by the Virginia Tech University Library suggests that there are four layers of digital literacy: learner; competencies; key values which include curiosity, reflection, equity and social justice, creativity, and participation; and multiple literacies which considers digital literacy as a metaliteracy that includes information, data, media, and invention literacies (See fig 1). Scholars of community engaged research might need to dig deeper into how various issues of access are intertwined with digital literacy. Carmen Kynard argues that "Connectivity, the nature of technological pedagogies, and racist schooling all intersect to reproduce the savage inequalities in which white wealthy schools prepares students for managerial roles [...] and poorer schools of color get computerized keyboarding and drill for the service industry" (332). Access to digital literacy is also determined by race and wealth, which further deepens the inequalities. Therefore, it is important to think of such literacies through a critical lens. Elaine Richardson reminds us that "Critical literacy is the search for truth through interrogating what we've been fed. We must ask ourselves who told us that and why? Who is empowered or disempowered by certain knowledge and social arrangements?" (11). Hence, critically thinking about digital technology and literacy from the perspective of access is not only important but also necessary. We need to continue to understand what roles we can play in the community where access to multiple elements of survival is limited. Hence, we need to continue questioning and challenging such forms of systems such that it allows us to critically think about the contexts in which digital access intertwines with multiple literacies.

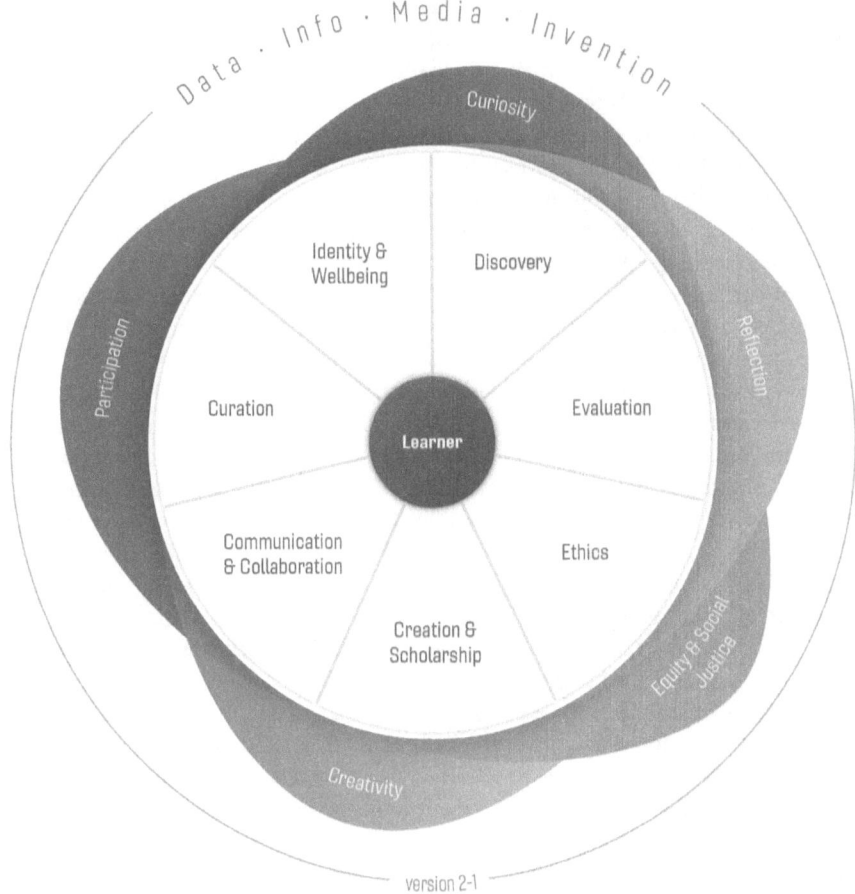

Figure 1 Digital Literacy Framework adapted from Virginia Tech Library's Digital Literacy Framework document

Building Equitable Partnerships Against Digital Divide

Scholars invested in the field of service learning and community engagement argue for intentionality, respect, serving the community and building equitable and sustainable partnerships with commitment to build communities (Bay and Swacha; Bernardo and Monberg; S. Parks). Such commitment of scholars according to Eric Hartman needs "enhanced intentionality with respect to what we claim, what we attempt, and how we speak about our various, related approaches to producing civic, student, community, institutional, and broadly public outcomes" (97). Such enhanced intentionality should be not only necessary but also required when we want to support communities who lack access to digital literacy. As universities advance innovation, technology, and reach beyond their physical and virtual boundaries, there is a need of consideration of who is denied access to literacies of such technological innovations and who is denied opportunity as a result of lack of access leading towards digital divide. Jan van Dijk notes that digital divide is framed primarily in terms of inequality of capabilities or skills which is often linked to the concept of literacy (6). Access in this context can refer to technological devices, connections, applications including the ability and digital literacy to use these devices (Dijk). Moreover, understanding digital literacy requires a transnational context as digital inclusion and participation are deeply entwined (Sharma et al.) and those who lack digital literacy and are excluded often represent historically and traditionally marginalized BIPOC communities that include immigrants and refugees. Hence, we need commitments towards building equitable partnerships that focus on providing accessibility to intentionally excluded populations within and beyond the university.

Tackling digital divide needs intentional partnership with the community that puts the need of the community's access, digital literacy, and the socio-economic aspects at the center. Community engaged scholars have focused on equitable partnerships as being reciprocal. Such reciprocity has been argued for more give-and-take format in university-community partnership (Cushman) which focuses more on negotiating power structures. Hence, it is a prime time to move towards a "social justice framework" that calls for ongoing reciprocity beyond the immediate partnerships that disrupts the conscious negotiations of power between academic institutions and community members (Bernardo and Monberg). Putting social justice frameworks at the front will allow scholars to think deeply about building equitable partnerships where intentionally excluded community are given space and their knowledge is valued and cared for. Bernardo and Monberg both argue that they see reciprocity as situated within a much longer timeframe that recognizes legacies of struggle, survival, collective resistance, and commitment (85). In the context of digitally excluded populations, digital literacy can't be achieved without socially just and equitable practices and partnerships that understands the lives, survival praxis, and resistance the excluded communities' practices. The equitable partnerships can be forged with grounding of intercultural communication that allows two different communities (for example students and excluded communities) and understand the differences and similarities. This will also go beyond the deficit perspective which is detrimental to building the equitable partnerships.

We need to build equitable partnerships with the community members who are denied access because of their geographical locations, language abilities, educational exposure, and socio-economic conditions. Such equity oriented social justice practices should help in getting deeper understanding of rhetorical situations, politics, cultural traditions, and listening to the community members on what has pushed them and their communities towards lack of digital literacy, access, and thus creating social inequity and injustice. Furthermore, by intentional partnerships building that incorporates social justice while working with an excluded community is very important for our students to understand how lack of access and digital literacy creates exclusion in the society. As the students prepare for their role especially in technical communication, they need to know and understand how they themselves with writing, research, and communication can impact communities in need. While building intentional partnerships, it is important for the students to understand that they need to engage without any preconceived notions about the community and going beyond the charity or deficit model of service learning. While they are engaged in such issue of equity and justice in mostly excluded communities, students need to develop intercultural awareness and know their audience by developing relationships and by reflecting on their own privileges as students in a land-grant institution. In the case of digital divide, students need a grounding on their own digital literacies and think deeper on their own privileges. This reflection will allow the students to ask uncomfortable questions with respect and providing promotion of cultural awareness that will be beneficial for the students in their future careers (Collopy).

Intentional Engagements: Local and Global Partnerships

In this section, I share the multidimensional aspects of access and digital literacy and how they intersect with each other and how intentional and equitable partnerships can be built by arguing for digital literacy as an issue of social justice. My journey of engaging with the community started back when I was in Nepal working as a communication practitioner via various non-profit based organizations. After a catastrophic earthquake, I engaged with many grassroots workers and activists as a disaster responder. During such experiences, I learned three things that would shape my identity as a community engagement scholar in my academic career: a) access and literacy are affected by deeply rooted social inequalities; b) partnerships can be built across time and space by putting the needs of the community first; and c) local and global resources could be sought and used via writing and communication for the benefit of the community. Later as a graduate student, I was introduced to community-based partnerships and work as a scholar and how such meaningful partnerships can support the communities. I learned that there are endless ways for a graduate student to be engaged within the community (Kumari; Hubrig). Engaging with the community by establishing partnerships allowed me as an international graduate student to become familiar with the community I was living in and it allowed me to connect my work with the social issues of that community such as food insecurity, ageing, and digital literacy (Hubrig et al.). I had limitless possibilities and endless exposure to community work and that created a ground for me to learn, work, and grow as a community engaged scholar. During this time, I learned how establishing a network with administration and being a liaison for the community is important to being an agent of change (Cushman). Below I share two different cases, a) partnership with Code for Nepal and b) partnership with Student Affairs at Virginia Tech University. Both partnerships focus on the issue of digital literacy and are intentional engagements.

Case #1

In the Spring of 2019, I met the CEO of Code for Nepal for an interview for my research, and when I learned about the organization's needs, I proposed a partnership between Code for Nepal and my business writing class that semester where the work that the students produced would be grounded in service learning and digital literacy. Code for Nepal's major goal is to enhance digital literacy among the rural and marginalized population in Nepal. Hence, digital literacy was at the core of this partnership and the major theme of my course. In this international service learning work, students supported the Code for Nepal's communication needs by developing a contextual understanding of how digital literacy intersects with issues such as gender, class, and caste in the case of Nepal. The students in the class and I applied for a grant and received $1,500 for Code for Nepal. The students not only engaged in understanding about the issue of digital literacy and issue of accessibility in Nepal but also to support the organization wrote grants and produced a plethora of items that I personally delivered to Nepal. This class took place in pre-Zoom era, but we used Skype in our class to organize virtual sessions from Nepal as well as from another state where the CEO lived. One of the students, Parul Chaube wrote, "one of the underlying goals of this class was global social justice […] and without physically being in Nepal, were able to impact the organizations' workshops and goals. This was probably the best learning experience we could obtain from semester-long class" (pg. 25). Therefore, the students' assignments constituted impactful work. This partnership illuminated the issues of access, power, and digital literacy and opened the endless possibilities for me as a scholar showing how a small work can be impactful. Thus, this partnership continued during the pandemic at Virginia Tech University. I have written about this partnership experience elsewhere (Baniya, Call, et al.; Baniya, Brein, et al.).

Case #2

The partnership with Code for Nepal led towards meaningful work as well as creating space in community engagement scholarship regarding access and issue of digital literacy as an issue of social justice. With enriched discussions and reflections in the class on digital literacy allowed a space to think about access from a multidimensional perspective. The lack of access to digital literacy and the ability to use digital devices has hindered the success of many individuals in not only Nepal but also within my new community in Blacksburg. After one semester long partnership and after curating a lot of digital products that are publicly accessible, it was time to think about partnerships in the local community in Blacksburg. Eventually, I came across the Literacy Volunteers of New River Valley which has been working towards community literacy in the New River Valley area in Southwest Virginia. The initial conversation about potential partnership led to some insightful conversation about the digital needs of the community where the organization needed more specific volunteers rather than a class partnership. Although the partnership didn't happen, I volunteered and supported the community partner. During the same meeting, I was informed about the daily struggles and digital needs of the staff at Virginia Tech who are pay band 1 or below which means that they are on the lowest pay standard or are working on wages without benefits and insurance. As a new member of this university and community, it was eye opening to know that a lot of immigrants and refugee population who have differing levels of literacies serve this university by doing jobs in the housekeeping department or the dining halls. Additionally, their struggle with language and digital literacy creates barrier to their success in their career. Smith argues that "the stakes of accessibility are therefore much higher than including disabled users or enabling aging-in-place: directing attention to the ways that socio-cultural and structural factors can limit access to technology is also critical" (153). Access of digital literacy in this population is determined by the socio-cultural, political, economic factors. Some members who have been part of reintegration to this community and specifically women were barred from education in their home countries and in the United States are dependent on either their husband or children to use technologies.

Listening to these struggles from the immigrant community, I shared what I had previously done with Code for Nepal. I was connected to the Student Affairs at Virginia Tech who was on board with a partnership to create user-based documentation targeting this specific population. My Fall 2021 Creating User Documentation class was great for this partnership which was different as the students were learning about and supporting the community members whom they might interact but may not know deeply. The community of people the class was targeting represented the marginalized community within this area, people from lower economic backgrounds, people who have immigrated to the U.S., and people who came to U.S. as refugees. In this class, our goal was to learn about the university staff that did not include administrators or professors. To reach this goal, students studied and explored that there is a plethora of information that one needs to consume as a university staff member and there are even more devices and digital technologies that one needs to know how to access to get that information. Moreover, the student affairs employees shared that due to language barriers, disability, education, and the economic status of the people who work these jobs (mostly the dining hall staff and the housekeeping staff), the staff members are often left behind when it comes to digital literacy. This information was shocking for the students who are majorly from a computer engineering background. The most uncomfortable was that there are plenty of resources that are available to these staff members, but due to their lack of digital literacy, education, or digital devices, these resources remain inaccessible among these community members. The question of who gets to access these resources and how continues to be problematic.

The Fall 2021 class started with direct communication with the staff from the dining halls at Virginia Tech. Due to their proximity to the community, the students conducted user-analysis by administering one-on-one interviews with the dining hall staff members. These interviews were challenging for the students and the staff both because of the language and technology barriers. It was important for the course that the students face these challenges which are the day to day for a lot of population who have lack of access. The assignment was not targeted towards getting perfect interview and perfect interview quotes but was to interact with the employees and really be in their shoes. For many students this was something that they have never done, and for many employees this was intimidating as they have never been interviewed about digital literacy capacities. As they reflected, the students admitted that they had a cross-cultural experience because they realized that the community they interviewed was completely different than the one they were from and thus had varied digital abilities. The information that someone is not able to perform tasks like opening email or opening up a browser was very shocking for students who grew up with technology. The students after this interview spent the entire semester curating user documentation and digital materials for the student affairs employees. This documentation aimed at providing the employees with resources that will allow them to utilize various digital products that are available to them on campus and that will help them navigate their daily life more easily. At the end of the semester, the students curated a public website which curated all the materials produced in the class. This class really pushed their boundaries towards understanding what access is, what their digital responsibility is, and how they can support these and similar communities. Students and I both have realized how digital literacy is so important to having access and how digitally literate community engaged scholars have a responsibility to tackle these issues.

In these two partnerships, over multiple semesters at two different institutions, the students have always found the concept of digital literacy as something new or not heard of until they themselves are posed with questions related with that. When the students get the firsthand information from the community members about and dig down deeper on the issue of digital divide, it has always been what the students call as an eye-opening issue. Most of the students in my class represent technologically advanced students who grew up with technology. Hence, something they always refer back to when they learn about digital divide is their own family and community where they have known their grandparents, neighbors, or people at church who struggle with digital issues. For students to get exposure to an international community lacking access, not knowing how to use computers changes their perspective about how unjust a society can be. In contrast to international community, visually seeing and talking about digital struggles of the community members within their own university is another opportunity for them to dig deeper on the unjust practices. The transnational context in both cases is important for the students to learn how digital divide is something that affects the most marginalized and even in the US. Students, who see first hand experience of struggles later mention that they have gained understanding of denial of access and opportunity based on digital literacy and why such divide should end. Some students have expressed desire to continue helping and supporting their own communities in their hometown or virtually volunteer and support communities across the world. These two classes have shown two things to the students, how it is also their responsibility to work towards the digital divide and ways that they can be helpful. While I don't claim that a few semesters worth of classes will end the systemic digital divide, these classes have helped in understanding digital literacy, access as an issue of social justice.

Digital Literacy, Accessibility & collective responsibility

The issue of digital literacy intersects with accessibility and various other issues of social justice including food, aging, and gender, and thus it is important to consider digital literacy from the lens of access and intersectionality. Likewise, people's abilities to access literacy is determined by various intersecting factors such as gender, economic status, and privilege. The systemic inequalities further restrict people's abilities to access literacy. The special issue editors, Hubrig & Cedillo, share in their call, "justice is impossible without our attunement to intersectionality." Intersectionality brings together ideas from disparate places, times, and perspectives, enabling people to share points of view that formerly were forbidden, outlawed, or simply obscured (Collins). Hence, it is our collective responsibility to think, research, and create space for discussing access and digital literacy. Furthermore, as Tabita Adkins argues, methodologies for studying community literacy should be reexamined considering advancements in technology and the research community's relationship to those technologies. Community engaged scholars need to consider digital literacy because the advancement, relationship, and access to technology and digital literacy will expose the context, realities, and ways one could participate in the community. In this way, the scholars can make gaps in the resources and access to those resources more visible and understand areas where their awareness and advocacy is most needed, further revealing the hidden resources or aspects (Fox). Adkins, whose research was within the Amish community, shares that, "In my world, the ability to produce and consume digital texts is at least normative if not expected. For the Amish, though, digital texts and the technology that creates and displays those texts are foreign, odd, and perhaps even dangerous" (1). Digital access and literacy are contextual to socio-cultural, political, and cultural identities and it is an issue that is often overlooked and taken for granted.

Digital literacy and access are a collective responsibility. Such collective responsibilities can be enacted by building intentional equitable partnerships with the community members. In the above sections, I have shown a multitude of issues of access that community engaged work can address and one of those is the issue of digital literacy as it is tied with how people access various elements in their life. As community engaged scholars, we have the ability to develop partnerships within our localities and beyond and many scholars have been creating an impact through their work. Scholars can create access and justice-oriented community literacy work which can support the marginalized populations and support them to gain various literacies including digital. As the world continues to go digital, there are higher chances of the digital divide creating gaps and inequities. We must rethink what access and literacy in community writing are and we must understand what our collective responsibilities are in this regard. Our positionalities as scholars of community engaged work provides us with certain privileges and positionalities that help us identify a variety of issues of access that are interconnected with race, gender, and identities. With this positionalities and critical thinking, we can develop intentional engagements and forge an equitable partnership that unravel the issue of digital literacy and accessibility other interconnected issues along with this issue. Rather than a give and take reciprocal engagements, intentional engagement regarding digital literacy allows to embrace social justice framework and helps to understand and tackle this issue in a multidimensional way.

Conclusion: Rethinking Access and Literacy in Community Writing

The concept of digital literacy in rhetoric and writing isn't new as scholars have worked towards thinking about how such literacies can improve classroom teaching. By centering our work around access and digital literacy, community engaged scholars can rethink about how inequalities and digital divide persists in the current contexts. The demands of digital literacies are so high in the current context that one to complete small daily task need to constantly engage with the digital environment. The lack of engagement in the digital environment creates hindrances in the success of the community people who are marginalized, who already have lack of access to the resources. Adhering to the current needs of the community, community engaged scholars need to think how multiple issues of access intersect with digital literacy. By rethinking access and literacy from the perspective of digital literacy allows community engaged scholars to think about access in a multidimensional way and how lack of access to digital literacy hinders multiple other literacies. Grounding access and literacy within the concepts of digital literacy allows scholars to think about identity, well-being, and ethics. Investment in digital literacy to explore what could be the ways to enhance multiple literacies via digital literacy will help in enhancing access and other forms of literacies.

Works Cited

Adkins, Tabetha. "Researching the 'Un-Digital' Amish Community: Methodological and Ethical Reconsiderations for Human Subjects Research." *Community Literacy Journal*, vol. 6, no. 1, Oct. 2011. *DOI.org (Crossref)*, https://doi.org/10.25148/CLJ.6.1.009405.

Baniya, Sweta, Kylie Call, et al. "COVID-19, International Partnerships, and the Possibility of Equity: Enhancing Digital Literacy in Rural Nepal amid a Pandemic – Reflections." *Reflections*, vol. 21, no. 1, 2022, https://reflectionsjournal.net/2022/02/covid-19-international-partnerships-and-the-possibility-of-equity-enhancing-digital-literacy-in-rural-nepal-amid-a-pandemic/.

Baniya, Sweta, Ashley Brein, et al. "International Service Learning in Technical Communication during a Global Pandemic." *Programmatic Perspective*, vol. 12, no. 2, 2021, pp. 26–58.

Bay, Jennifer L., and Kathryn Yankura Swacha. "Community-Engaged Research as Enmeshed Practice." *Michigan Journal of Community Service Learning*, vol. 26, no. 1, 2020, pp. 121–42.

Beaunoyer, Elisabeth, et al. "COVID-19 and Digital Inequalities: Reciprocal Impacts and Mitigation Strategies." *Computers in Human Behavior*, vol. 111, Oct. 2020, p. 106424. *PubMed Central*, https://doi.org/10.1016/j.chb.2020.106424.

Bernardo, Shane, and Terese Guinsatao Monberg. "Resituating Reciprocity within Longer Legacies of Colonization: A Conversation." *Community Literacy Journal*, vol. 14, no. 1, 2019, p. 89-93.

Cedillo, Christina V. "Disabled and Undocumented: In/Visibility at the Borders of Presence, Disclosure, and Nation." *Rhetoric Society Quarterly*, vol. 50, no. 3, 2020, pp. 203–11. DOI.org (Crossref), https://doi.org/10.1080/02773945.2020.1752131.

Chaube, Parul. "Importance and Challenges of International Service-Learning." *Purdue Journal of Service-Learning and International Engagement*, vol. 7, no. 1, 2020, pp. 19–27. DOI.org (Crossref), https://doi.org/10.5703/1288284317230.

Collopy, Rachel M. B., Sharon Tjaden-Glass, & Novea A. McIntosh. "Attending to Conditions That Facilitate Intercultural Competence." *Michigan Journal of Community Service Learning*, vol. 26, no. 1, Winter 2020, pp. 19-38.

Collins, Patricia Hill. Intersectionality As Critical Social Theory. Duke University Press, 2019.

Crenshaw, Kimberlé Williams. "Intersectionality, Identity Politics and Violence Against Women of Color." Kvinder, Køn & Forskning, no. 2–3, 2006. *DOI.org (Crossref)*, https://doi.org/10.7146/kkf.v0i2-3.28090.

Cushman, Ellen. "The Rhetorician as an Agent of Social Change." *College Composition and Communication*, vol. 47, no. 1, Feb. 1996, p. 7. Crossref, https://doi.org/10.2307/358271.

Dijk, Jan van. *The Digital Divide*. John Wiley & Sons, 2020

Dobson, Teresa M., and John Willinsky. "Digital Literacy." The Cambridge Handbook of Literacy. Ed. David R. Olson and Nancy Torrance. Cambridge: Cambridge UP, 2009. 286-312. Print. Cambridge Handbooks in Psychology.

Espejel, Alondra Kiawitl, Mariano Espinoza, Louis Mendoza, and Martha Ockenfels-Martinez. "A Dream Deffered?: Building Activists for Educational Justice, Access, and Equity." *Reflections*, vol. 8, no.2, 2009, p. 31-61

Fox, Kathy R. "Exploring Literacy In Our Own Backyard: Increasing Teachers' Understanding of Literacy Access through Community Mapping." *Journal of Praxis in Multicultural Education*, vol. 8, no. 2, Jan. 2014. *DOI.org (Crossref)*, https://doi.org/10.9741/2161-2978.1071.

Hartman, Eric. "A Strategy for Community-Driven Service-Learning and Community Engagement: Fair Trade Learning." *Michigan Journal of Community Service Learning*, vol. 22, no. 1, 2015, p. 97-100.

House, Veronica. "Re-Framing the Argument: Critical Service- Learning and Community-Centered Food Literacy." *Community Literacy Journal*, vol. 8, no. 2, Apr. 2014. *DOI.org (Crossref)*, https://doi.org/10.25148/CLJ.8.2.009307.

Hubrig, Ada, Katie McWain, Marcus Meade, & Rachael W. Shah. "Positionality and Possibility: Reframing Tactics and Strategies for Graduate Student Community Engagement." *Michigan Journal of Community Service Learning*, vol. 24, no. 1, Nov. 2017. *DOI.org (Crossref)*, https://doi.org/10.3998/mjcsloa.3239521.0024.108.

Hubrig, Ada. "'We Move Together:' Reckoning with Disability Justice in Community Literacy Studies." *Community Literacy Journal*, vol. 14, no. 2, Dec. 2020. *DOI.org (Crossref)*, https://doi.org/10.25148/14.2.009042.

—. *Preparing Citizens, Composing Publics: Composition Pedagogy as a Primer for Engaged Citizenship.* The University of Nebraska - Lincoln. *ProQuest*, https://www.proquest.com/docview/2436435831/abstract/721D762B5D654BF0PQ/1. Accessed 14 Mar. 2022.

Kannan, Vani, et al. "Unmasking Corporate-Military Infrastructure: Four Theses." *Community Literacy Journal*, vol. 11, no. 1, 2016, pp. 76–93.

Kavensky, Kara. "The Importance of Digital Literacy." *Indianapolis Recorder*, 26 Feb. 2021, https://indianapolisrecorder.com/the-importance-of-digital-literacy/.

Kumari, Ashanka. "Community Engagement for the Graduate Student Soul: Ruminations on Reflections." *Reflections*, vol. 20, no. 1, 2020, pp. 122-131. https://reflectionsjournal.net/2020/09/community-engagement-for-the-graduate-student-soul-ruminations-on-reflections-by-ashanka-kumari/.

Kynard, Carmen. "'Wanted: Some Black Long Distance [Writers]': Blackboard Flava-Flavin and Other AfroDigital Experiences in the Classroom." *Computers and Composition*, vol. 24, no. 3, Jan. 2007, pp. 329–45. *DOI.org (Crossref)*, https://doi.org/10.1016/j.compcom.2007.05.008.

Mathieu, Paula. "The Contemplative Concerns of Community Engagement: What I Wish I Knew about the Work of Community Writing Twenty Years Ago." *Community Literacy Journal*, vol. 14, no. 2, Oct. 2020, pp. 38-48.

Mathieu, Paula, and Diana George. "Not Going It Alone: Public Writing, Independent Media, and the Circulation of Homeless Advocacy." *College Composition and Communication*, vol. 61, no. 1, 2009, pp. 130–49. *Zotero*, http://www.jstor.org/stable/40593519.

Manandhar, Asmita. "Midlife Education: Women Beating Illiteracy." *EducateNepal*, https://www.educatenepal.com/education_issues/display/midlife-education-women-beating-illiteracy. Accessed 14 Mar. 2022.

Parks, Stephen J. "Strategic Speculations on the Question of Value: The Role of Community Publishing in English Studies." *College English*, vol. 71, no. 5, 2009, pp. 506–27. *JSTOR*, http://www.jstor.org/stable/25652988.

—. "Sinners Welcome: The Limits of Rhetorical Agency." *College English*, vol. 76, no. 6, 2014, pp. 506–24. *JSTOR*, http://www.jstor.org/stable/24238200.

Powell, Katrina M. *Identity and Power in Narratives of Displacement.* Routledge, 2015. *www-taylorfrancis-com.ezproxy.lib.vt.edu*, https://doi.org/10.4324/9781315727141.

Richardson, Elaine. "'She Ugly': Black Girls, Women in Hiphop and Activism—Hiphop Feminist Literacies Perspectives." *Community Literacy Journal*, vol. 11, no. 1, Fall. 2021, p. 23.

Sen, Sandeep. "Illiteracy, Old Policies Hurdles for 'Digital Nepal' - The Himalayan Times - Nepal's No.1 English Daily Newspaper | Nepal News, Latest Politics, Business, World, Sports, Entertainment, Travel, Life Style News." *The Himalayan Times*, 8 Apr. 2019, https://thehimalayantimes.com/business/illiteracy-old-policies-hurdles-for-digital-nepal.

Shah, Rachael W. "'What Is It That's Going on Here?': Community Partner Frames for Engagement." *Community Literacy Journal*, vol. 14, no. 2, 2, Oct. 2020, pp. 72-92.

Sharma, Ravi, et al. "Digital Literacy and Knowledge Societies: A Grounded Theory Investigation of Sustainable Development." *Telecommunications Policy*, vol. 40, no. 7, July 2016, pp. 628–43. *DOI.org (Crossref)*, https://doi.org/10.1016/j.telpol.2016.05.003.

Stoecker, Randy, and Elizabeth Tryon. "Unheard Voices: Community Organizations and Service Learning." *The Unheard Voices*, edited by Randy Stoecker et al., Temple University Press, 2009, pp. 1-18. *JSTOR*, http://www.jstor.org/stable/j.ctt1bw1j7m.4.

Swacha, Kathryn Yankura. "Service-Learning in the Second Language Writing Classroom: Future Directions for Research." *TESOL Journal*, vol. 9, no. 2, 2018, pp. 278–98. *Wiley Online Library*, https://doi.org/10.1002/tesj.321.

Author Bio

Dr. Sweta Baniya is an assistant professor of rhetoric and professional and technical writing and an affiliate faculty of the Center for Coastal Studies at Virginia Polytechnic Institute and State University. Through a transnational and non-Western perspective, her research focusses on transnational coalitions in disaster response, crisis communication, and non-western rhetorics. She is working on her first book-length project *Transnational Assemblages: Social Justice Oriented Technical Communication in Global Disaster Management* where she explores transnational activism in the April 2015 Nepal Earthquake and 2017 Hurricane Maria in Puerto Rico. Email: baniya@vt.edu

Reinventing a Cultural Practice of Interdependence to Counter the Transnational Impacts of Disabling Discourses

Elenore Long

Abstract

The women's talking group featured in this article theorizes the community literacy practice of thanduk—"setting something aside"—that members practice together. Sanduk—with an s and translated as Arabic for "box"— has a long, well documented history involving informal, rotary credit and savings associations practiced among people in Africa and of African descent. Rather than using the s, the group's spelling is distinctively Nuer— thanduk—harkening back to indigenous versions of the practice documented throughout areas of East Africa and beyond. Thanduk invokes nommo, a distinctly African spiritual and philosophical value that strives for harmony and balance among interdependent members of a community. This article aims to make legible how the women in this study employ thanduk to thwart the transnational, intergenerational impacts of indirect colonial rule and neoliberal economics in pursuit of individual and collective thriving.

Keywords

access, community literacy, indirect colonial rule, mobility, mutual thriving, neoliberal economics, women's empowerment

The women's talking group featured in this article theorizes the community literacy practice of thanduk—"setting something aside"—that members practice together to wrangle the disabling discourses of indirect colonial rule and neoliberal economics in pursuit of individual and collective thriving. Featured in this study, the women who practice thanduk together are an ethnically diverse group of Nuer, Dinka and Arab women who work at a hair braiding salon owned by a South Sudanese refugee named Ruth. Significantly, thanduk requires mutual trust and investment among the braiders, including those who are members of communities elsewhere positioned as mortal enemies (Mamdani 213-18). For the women at the shop, the practice of thanduk goes like this: Every other Saturday, each of the ten women pitches in $300 in cash; the women take turns cashing in the pot of money—individually setting aside the $3000 when it's their respective turn. At the salon, thanduk operates in an economy of scarcity. Typically, a woman might cobble together her cash for thanduk from one or two other part-time gigs, as well as her job at the salon.

Cash from thanduk is usually insufficient for eradicating the problems towards which the braiders put their money. But one of the first things you learn at the shop is that despair is not an option. Women profess deep satisfaction and joy in coming together to invest in one another's lives this way. The possibility of an invitation to join the thanduk circle is one of the main draws of working at the salon. In light of this vitality, this study asks:

- How can the practice of thanduk be understood in relation not only to disabling discursive forces that the women and their families navigate daily, but also to the women's persistence, often against great odds? and
- What inspiration can community literacy find for our own efforts to engage with community partners—inspiration that avoids misappropriating the cultural practice of thanduk but takes critical lessons from it?

With an s̩ and translated as Arabic for "box" (*Encyclopaedia of Islam*), ṣandūḵ has a long, well documented history involving informal, rotary credit and savings associations practiced among people in Africa and of African descent (Ardener; Geertz; Osondu). Rather than using the s̩, the group's spelling is distinctively Nuer—*thanduk*—harkening back to indigenous versions of the practice documented throughout areas of East Africa and beyond (Ardener 204-08) and invoking the distinctly African spiritual and philosophical value of nommo that strives for harmony and balance among interdependent members of a community (see Alkebulan 51). So this spelling is followed here, as well. This article aims to make legible how the women in this study employ thanduk to thwart the transnational, intergenerational impacts of disabling discourses.

To study thanduk is also to acknowledge a limitation: here at the salon, you need capital, an invitation, and staying power to participate. This bias creates a built-in barrier to access. Yet community literacy projects are often in a position to address such barriers; for instance, by devising equitable, collaboratively constructed processes for distributing resources for BIPOC youth-based outdoor justice initiatives like Atabey Outdoors (Blandin), community restoration projects like 17Strong's urban renewal initiative (Simmons "Attending") and environmental projects like those sponsored by the Southwest Environmental Education Coalition (Kells). This study considers how thanduk could inform the design of other such collaboratives.

I. Indirect Rule and Neoliberal Economics Collude to Restrict Access and Mobility

Indirect rule and neoliberal economics collude to restrict the access and mobility of refugees. Doing so, these discourses threaten to disable material conditions for hope. Three cases (textboxes 1-3) help to expose the havoc these discourses wreak on people's lives.

Indirect Rule: The Disabling Effects of Restricted Access

What makes the civil war period in Sudan from 1983-2005 particularly tragic is that for thousands of years and for all their differences, the peoples of current-day Sudan and South Sudan "cohabitated and shared the land" with peoples different from themselves (Zambakari, "South Sudan" 106). African Studies scholar Christopher Zambakari notes: "Historically, political and economic conditions moved people from one region to another. ... Sudan never had a demarcated border with its neighbors and people moved freely between regions and states" (107). For example, cattle herders who lived on "semi-permanent agricultural settlements" made room when nomadic herders came through on their "seasonal pattern of migration" to find water (Mamdani qtd. in Zambakari 107). Several forces colluded to produce the bloody and protracted civil war to which the study's participants lost family members and relatives and from which they fled as refugees. Forces fueling the conflict included the "political, social, and economic marginalization of the peripheries, the role of religion in the state, ... forced Arabization and Islamization, mismanagement of diversity, national crisis of identity, and the institutional legacy of [British] colonialism" (Zambakari 89).

Taking over Sudan in the early 20th century, British colonial rule deliberately fomented the interethnic conflict leading to the civil war period in Sudan from 1983-2005 and undermining nation-building efforts in South Sudan thereafter. *Direct* British colonial rule extracted resources from Sudan, exporting and exploiting them for the benefit of the British empire. *Indirect* British colonial rule controlled and shrank the resources available to the native people of Sudan. Particularly ruthless, this strategy took resources left scarce after Britain plundered them for the empire's gain, and made access to them contingent on one's affiliation with the ethnic group deemed the majority of a given region. This strategy weaponized ethnic differences by dispensing resources to particular tribes while denying resources to others, pitting tribes against one another on the basis of what had previously been cultural but not political differences. Mahmood Mamdani recounts the consequence: "Residents deemed native understood that it was through tribe and tribe alone that they could legitimately organize to make demands from the colonial state, and so it is perfectly understandable that tribe became a politically meaningful category to the people themselves" (214). Consider what indirect rule meant—how it played out—in the Murle district of Jonglei, one of ten states in South Sudan. Prior to colonization, the region had been home to six ethnic groups: "Nuer, Dinka, Anyuak, Murle, Kachipo and Jieh, all peoples with long histories of mobility within the territory" (Mamdani 249). But under colonialism, only those deemed the ethnic majority within a given region had "customary rights to resources from which minorities were excluded" (249). "[I]s it any wonder," Mamdani asks, "that conflict would arise?" (249).

Civil war in Sudan—like any other war—has produced disability. The physical violence of war itself is to blame; and so, too, are the ways that war limits access to necessary resources such as decent affordable food, shelter, stable internet, clean water, and health care. These restrictions carry their own disabling consequences. As Nirmala Erevelles argues in *Disability and Difference in Global Contexts: Enabling a Transformative Body Politic*, "To put it simply, war is one of the largest producers of disability in a world that is still inhospitable to disabled people" (132). Taking the war on terror in Afghanistan as a case in point, Erevelles traces such reverberations. Her analysis begins by documenting ways that war produced disability in those wounded in war: "loss of limbs, paralysis, emotional trauma" (137). She then observes that war further disables by destroying the infrastructure by which communities would have otherwise accessed resources. These disabling effects extend to refugees. Erevelles documents that "Afghan refugees wounded and/or disabled as a result of 'friendly fire' have had to depend on the meager resources of their families for survival" (137). The full toll includes the "disproportionate surge in the numbers of children and adults with disabilities as a result of war-related injuries, military torture, civil war, economic scarcities, and psychological trauma" (144). A primary way that war disables is by restricting civilians' access to material resources. In Afghanistan, for instance, "access to disability services for women is very limited, and during Taliban rule these services ceased functioning. Even community rehabilitation is restricted for women and children" (137).

The consequences of war in Sudan—one set of British colonialism's disabling effects —continue to reverberate eight thousand miles away in Phoenix, Arizona. The case in textbox 1 drives this point home.

Indirect Rule's Disabling Consequences: The Case of Ailith's Placement in Special Education

Ailith was recently placed in a self-contained special education classroom though she has no documented learning disability. She was raised in a refugee camp in Ethiopia with her mother. For years, her uncle and her aunt Oriana—a braider at Ruth's shop—had petitioned for Ailith and her mother to come live with them to improve their life chances. Finally, Ailith was able to join Oriana and her family though Ailith's mother is still in a refugee camp in Ethiopia. Yet, after relocating to the US, circumstances remain daunting. In her new school in Phoenix, Ailith was deemed a high school junior, but because she received little schooling at the refugee camp where she spent her childhood, she was placed in a special education program with minimal opportunities to interact with the larger student body. To be clear, in the center of the city, the Phoenix School District has state-of-the-art programs for refugee children. But on the city's outskirts where Oriana and her family can afford housing, the district's current austerity measures preclude such accommodations. As a consequence, developmentally appropriate instruction—including formal, sustained English as a Second Language reading instruction—is not accessible to Ailith. Furthermore, possibilities of meaningful post-graduation employment are limited since she struggles to read. (talking group session (TGS) 4/17/2019)

Textbox 1. Example of a disabling consequence of indirect rule

Erevelles's argument speaks to Ailith's placement in special education by exposing how, within educational systems here in the US, disproportionate numbers of "students marked oppressively by race, class, gender, and sexuality are dis-located into the postcolonial ghettoes of alternative schooling" (93). The material consequences can be enormously harmful, including lower rates of graduation, fewer opportunities for economically meaningful work, and greater likelihood of moving through the school-to-prison pipeline for students so dis-located. As Ailith and her aunt are well-aware, the long-term material consequences of this repeated treatment can be "horribly damaging," as Erevelles notes, including the possibility of "becoming completely alienated from the labor market and the wider social world" (67).

Neoliberal Economics: The Disabling Effects of Forestalled Mobility

When framed expansively, mobility is a dynamic, experiential and shared socio-political phenomenon that simultaneously relies on and produces infrastructure. Expansive movement is "a form of hope, a manner of trying" (Dolmage, "Mapping" 24). In disability studies, infrastructure that anticipates the full, changing array of human mobilities is referred to as universal design; such infrastructure allows people to move through space together unimpeded by physical, metaphysical and/or social architecture (Dolmage "Steep Steps"). Especially significant to thanduk as practiced in this study, this infrastructure merges people and the tools they use to coordinate movement through space; the example of the Ashby BART Station in Berkeley, California, demonstrates how tools-in-use distribute and network traction.

The focal point at the Ashby BART Station is a large, red cantilevered 'helical' ramp. In "Steep Steps," Jay Dolmage cites the ramp as an example of "proactive" design that literally embodies "future possibilities" *as people put it to use* (110). The ramp illustrates that 1) mobility is a shared responsibility, not primarily a private matter; 2) people employ inherently diverse embodiments in order to move; and 3) movement isn't intrinsically linear but also side-ways, iterative, networked, and kairotic. In other words, tools-in-use such as the Ashby BART station's helical ramp allow "[t]he contingent and provisional management of the present opportunity" ("Breathe" 121). Tools-in-use embody "the capacity to act in a kairotic world" and enact the "speculatively mobile form of interpretation" necessary to act in the moment (White qtd. in Dolmage, "Breathe" 121). Unlike steep steps that impede people with limited mobility, or retrofitted fixes that attempt to facilitate mobility through architectural add-ons, universal design promotes expansive instantiations of mobility. Infrastructure, Dolmage contends, is constituted in the unfolding feat of such movement.

Neoliberal forces conspire to forestall mobility, as the women's empowerment meeting featured in textbox 2 demonstrates. As the impetus for the meeting, women's empowerment served as an umbrella category for services supporting women in Phoenix's South Sudanese community. Several years ago now, a fellow named Tap Dak, the outreach coordinator from the Lost Boys Center in town, came to campus to recruit volunteers to support such services. Responding to his invitation, my colleague Jennifer Clifton and I started volunteering at the center. He also invited us to attend women's empowerment networking meetings in order to get to know women in the community. It was at the meeting described below that many of us in the talking group first met.

Neoliberalism's Disabling Moral Code: The Case of the Women's Empowerment Meeting

Hundreds of women from Phoenix's South Sudanese community streamed into the hall that afternoon to discuss something they all needed if they were to contribute to their families' incomes: day care for their children. The male community leaders had called the meeting because of the urgency of the matter. And while they had the women gathered, these leaders announced that they would call a vote before the meeting was out to determine whether the eleven women presiding over the community's women-led leadership council would continue operating independently, or if the council would be subsumed under the governance of the community's male leadership. The unstated warrant for the vote was that the women's leadership council had dropped the ball, foremost by not solving the community's day care problem.

Under the first item of business, two guest speakers highlighted relevant social services under their purview. The director of the Arizona Refugee Resettlement Program recounted welfare services in place for refugees—services that expire after their first five years in the state. *In light of these services, what did the women have to show for themselves?* A Somali man described a successful initiative to create culturally sustaining day care for a population of Somali living in the heart of Phoenix. *Why hadn't the Sudanese women created something similar?* In the discussion that ensued, the guest speakers and the men in the room made claims on the women's time, energy, relationships, and resources: earn money, be a good mother, own and run a small business, get an education, visit sick elders, teach your children your native language, improve your English, attend three-hour meetings regularly, cook meals for several hundred people in the name of group cohesion, stay to clean up afterward, send money to family, and so on. Implicitly, these claims criticized the South Sudanese women for failing to leverage the state's services toward the community's resettlement. *Why hadn't they done more? Why were many in the community still struggling so?*

Speaking in one or more of five different languages, individual women in the audience responded—some dependent on translators from the Sudanese Mission Church to translate between Dinka and English. The women in the room who spoke primarily either Arabic or Nuer were left to their own devices to follow along and contribute as best they could. A woman who introduced herself as Anguma was the first to speak: "Your first task as a refugee is a job. You must get a job. You work to have a place to live, for food and clothes, for your family, to survive. Before you know it, five years has elapsed. When you open your eyes, time has really gone" (meeting notes, July 18, 2010). Jen would later write, the women "spoke of changing jobs every few months in search of better pay, daytime hours, better working conditions, and a location closer to where they were living at the time. Day-to-day tasks of making their way across Phoenix's urban sprawl; doing hours of repetitive manual labor; caring for children..." (Clifton, "Mastery" 241).

As the meeting continued, the temperature in the room rose, and the atmosphere in the room grew increasingly tense. The male president motioned to call for a vote whether to subsume the organizational structure of the women's leadership council under the community's male-led umbrella organization. Jen and I paid special attention, then, when in the culminating moments of this long, hot, tense meeting, the presiding leader of the women's council walked to the front of the room, took the microphone, and addressed the group: "I resign." One by one, the ten other members of the women's leadership council likewise made her way to the microphone and stated, "I resign." (women's empowerment meeting 7/18/2010)

Textbox 2. Example of neoliberalism's moral code forestalling mobility

Shrinking the public sphere while casting resources as charity. As is evident in Anguma's testimony, a refugee is under extreme pressure to "reduce his or her burden on society, and instead to build up his or her own human capital—in other words, to 'be an entrepreneur of her/himself'" (Ong 13). Refugee resettlement discourse normalizes the neoliberal entrepreneurial premise of the hustle—a racialized relationship to labor, precisely being Black and "forced to work incessantly [...] with no role in the formal economy [and] with no way out" (Spence 2). In a recent newsletter, Arizona Department of Health Service characterized resettlement as a process marked by "uncertainty, social isolation, *hustling* to support your family and the steep learning curve of acculturation" (1; emphasis added). Yet the market renders economic self-sufficiency ever elusive. As Sara McKinnon puts it, "The oppositional position to the citizen-subject constructs refugees in a continual state of transition, never quite intelligible as fully citizens" (397). Refugees—as Anguma attests—work hard to earn recognition as full citizens, but low-paying jobs keep them dependent on state services, dependence that undermines their claims to full citizenship.

Maintaining this entrepreneurial premise, neoliberalism then "shrinks the public sphere" by taking off the table matters of "collective caretaking" (Duggan 22, 88). Prevailing talk at the women's empowerment meeting blamed the women—as people receiving services—for failing the South Sudanese community as well as the state when their lives proved more complicated than the logic and mechanisms of resettlement assume. This blame-game preserved the status of the welfare director and the men in the room as the experts while laying blame at the women's feet for the actual difficulties that come with resettling in the US as a refugee. This stop-gap approach to public service is none other than retrofitting. Sure, problems with infrastructure can still expose structural elements that aren't working. But rather than resolving those structural issues, retrofitted stop-gaps merely cover them over. Working in this way, retrofitting "obscures differences" and "reinforces the status quo" while obstructing mobility of people who don't fit the pre-established standards required for unobstructed movement (Kerschbaum qtd. in Dolmage, "Steep Steps" 111). In the case featured in textbox 2, the state's retrofitted services obscured significant differences in the resettlement policies that relocated distinct populations of Somali and South Sudanese refugees at different points in the city's recent history—while implying that these one-size-fits-all services should be sufficient to cover everyone's needs, regardless of how different they may be.[4]

Excluding epistemic insight in public while indicting the moral character of those "in need." Epistemic exclusion perpetrates "a social injustice ... that cascades from the denial of other people's humanity and, by extension, a refusal to recognise their epistemic virtue" (Ndlovu-Gatsheni 887). As the women at the empowerment meeting knew perfectly well, they have firsthand experiences with conditions of forced migration—spanning from their past to very recent memories of their own lives and the lives of others whom they know and care about (Clifton "Feminist Collaboratives"; Long and Kang). Their experiences were relevant sources of knowledge for solving problems, including those that spurred the men to call the meeting (textbox 2). Yet in decision-making conversations with the state, the women were denied what Michele Simmons terms "public epistemological status" (*Participation* 33).

Particularly insulting—members of the women's leadership council would tell Jen and me later—was the indictment of their moral character for the ostensible failings of the community. The women who resigned from their positions chafed at the presumption that *if you can't secure self-sufficiency under prevailing economic conditions, the problem lies with you—your time management, your poor decisions, all matters of your moral character. Since you are on the receiving side of the charity, your job is to make the retrofitting work.* By denying "the actual processes of life and the conditions for existence," this moral indictment belies one of the most "seductive aspects of coloniality," observes Ndjovu-Gatsheni: "its time-perfected strategy of always masquerading as a civilizing [in this case moral-character-building] enterprise while in reality [being] a death project" (888). The hypocrisy of this moral positioning fuels the righteous indignation of angry youth in the community. Such troubled teenagers become sources of deep concern for mothers in the talking group. It breaks their hearts to see their disaffected teenagers enact paralogical critiques of neoliberalism's death grip. The moms worry that this critique is not productive but instead foments corrosive attitudes and behaviors (textbox 3).

The Specter of "Slow Death" Under Neoliberalism: The Case of Nyayoi's Teen Daughter

Teenagers are well aware—the women note at a recent talking group—that being on welfare means you're always under the thumb of the state. As moms and aunts, they consider what to tell teenagers when they ask why their fathers and uncles with advanced degrees still need food stamps and rent subsidies to raise their families; why the work their fathers and uncles most often find are in low-wage human-sector positions surveilling other Black or Brown bodies in the pe-

> nal or foster care systems. It worries the women intensely when disaffected teens actively refuse to participate in family life and school. As mothers, they express feelings of culpability, having left their children largely to raise themselves in what feels like a strange, inhospitable culture.
>
> Nyayoi's eldest daughter, for instance, started rebelling during her last years of high school. She refused to help with her younger siblings, and frankly Nyayoi didn't want her attitude rubbing off on them. Poor attendance kept her from walking at graduation; she refused to look for a job or sign up for community college, even though her parents had made doing so a condition of her having a car. For a particularly intense period of time, she didn't come home at night, leaving Nyayoi and her husband to worry about the company she was keeping and the very real possibility that poor decisions could jeopardize her safety and even land her in jail.
>
> Psychologists refer to the dilemma as "the immigrant paradox." Here, second-generation immigrants fare worse than their parents. In such cases, "time spent in [the] new country ... compound[s] the effects of migration and assimilation challenges and lead[s] to deteriorated mental health" (Stark et al. 20). In their 2022 study, Nhial Tutlam—himself a member of the South Sudanese community—and his colleagues found that US-born children of South Sudanese parents suffer from significantly higher rates of depression, antisocial behavior, anxiety and aggressive behaviors than other immigrant youth.
>
> A final resort for youth who have tested these parents' last nerves, mothers pay costly airfare to send beloved teens to family in Ethiopian resettlement centers in hopes of helping their kids find traction for charting their lives into adulthood. In early 2020, on the advice of her brother, a psychologist specializing in South Sudanese resettlement who had done similarly for his own son, Nyayoi used her thanduk money to send her eldest daughter to live with aunts and a dying grandmother outside Addis Ababa, Ethiopia—the same extended family to whom Nyayoi has been sending remittances each month since becoming a braider in the US. (TGS 10/9/2021)

Textbox 3: Example of the specter of "slow death" under neoliberalism

The talking group members' teenage children don't need academic theory to feel in their bones the threat of perpetual subjugation. They rage at US culture for extracting their parents' lifeblood, rendering Black bodies disposable and personhood primarily economic. For academic readers, the concept of "slow death" may illuminate how neoliberal logic exacerbates colonialism's "death project" (Ndjovu-Gatsheni 888). Citing to Lauren Berlant's *Cruel Optimism*, Dolmage opens up this perverse vortex for theorizing. "Slow death," he writes, describes the embodied consequences of hope perpetually deferred, he explains. Most cruel, slow death indicts "populations marked out for wearing out" (Berlant qtd. in Dolmage, "Steep Steps" 108). For youth like Nyayoi's daughter and nephew, the ruse—that their parents could somehow hustle hard enough to get the state off their back—is up. They are acutely aware that their parents' struggles portend adult difficulties of their own.

II. The *How* of the Talking Group: The Rhetoricity Confirming Nyayoi's Hunch

The ideas presented in this article are shared with talking-group members' written permission. Pseudonyms are used throughout to protect their own and family members' confidentiality, including, importantly, the women's financial sovereignty. So, what's *the how* of the talking group? How did we get here? This section turns to African studies scholarship to account for the rhetoricity—the reverberating call and response—that has networked the practice of thanduk to the talking group, the very rhetoricity that has made this article possible.

The talking group operates on the basis of a real but tacit social contract in addition to the paperwork required by the university review board where I work. After the women's empowerment meeting culminated in the women leaders' resignations (textbox 2), a South Sudanese participant at the meeting named Julia nominated the idea of a talking group to support women's empowerment—informal meetings that could happen in lots of languages and for which school literacy would *not* be an entrance requirement (Long and Kang). Subsequently, Nyayoi sent me a message on WhatsApp: she felt something special was happening with her community practice of thanduk, and she wondered if a talking group could both support Julia's initiative and let me, as a community literacy researcher/writer, learn about this practice. On the evenings designated for thanduk when the braiders have hung back for the talking group, Nyayoi has led the conversation—issuing each time an open invitation to stay and talk as you like—to share what you like—and to leave when you want or need to get going. Meanwhile, Nyayoi and Oriana have endorsed my presence in relation to more than a decade of previous collaboration (Long et al.). Nyayoi has positioned me at the salon to listen, as well as to embody the reality of other public workers who might find value in what she and the other women in the talking group wish to share. Her hunch—that thanduk was something I needed to learn about and that a thanduk-specific talking group could be my entrance point—has proven correct, as this article attests.

Scholarship from African studies helps articulate the conditions under which and the means by which the talking group has sustained itself. The problem decolonizing work poses is foremost a *how* question, Shose Kessi et al. contend. "The problem has been *not knowing how to do this together, how* to escape the entrapments and dilemmas of our epicolonial system" (276; emphasis added). This means attempts are bound to be aspirational—imperfect efforts at navigating vibrant but also often volatile differences; ghastly histories; and warped, self-interested institutional logics in order to come together for newly imagined purposes. In this regard, "Cognitive Empire" offers direction. Sabelo Ndlovu-Gatsheni observes that "struggles for decolonisation" are taking place "across the world" (895) wherever "[r]acism, patriarchy, sexism, Eurocentrism, and capitalist logics of exploitation are once more put in the public space for critique" (895). Taking cues from Ndlovu-Gatsheni's call, what follows accounts for how the talking group has produced the rhetorical alchemy confirming Nyayoi's hunch.

The talking group sustains itself by . . .

- **valuing thanduk as a public practice and as a practice of a public.** The public quality of sanduk has been documented historically. In fact, in her landmark comparative study of rotating credit associations, Shirley Ardener translates the term in Mba-Ise for these associations—oha—as "public," as in a "(public) contribution" (204). In and beyond the collection and distribution of cash contributions, the talking group attests to something less available to Ardener and her network of fellow anthropologists: the co-constitutive publicness of thanduk. That is, the practice of thanduk produces a public; and simultaneously—as the practice is enacted—this local public practices its mutual commitment to its members publicly. In this regard, thanduk is not only an informal economic system of social significance; it also actively and protractedly produces infrastructure to support mutual thriving. The talking group sustains itself by valuing this work.
- **theorizing public-literacy work on the basis of African experiences and histories** (Asante; Kershaw). Foremost, this means members of the talking group attend to one another's insights on each woman's terms, rather than against some imported expectation of what qualifies as a good idea. This premise embodies Selena Rodgers's call in "Womanism and Afrocentricity: Understanding the Intersection" for knowledge-building approaches that "accentuate constructs that emphasize Black women's intrinsic need for self-definition, self-valuation, name, and reaffirming Afrocentric analysis in everyday experiences" (37).

    For me, this mode includes turning critically on disciplinary concepts of public life predicated on "European and North American experiences" (Ndlovu-Gatsheni 892). Imperialist disciplinary assumptions need to be "unlearn[ed]," write Kessi et al. (271). Foremost among assumptions to be unlearned, argues Zambakari in "Challenges of Liberal Peace," is that the institutions of modern liberal democracies are themselves either inherently beneficent or necessary for the production of peace—and, thus, appropriate blueprints or gold standards for theorizing public life in Africa (and by extension, for studying a public practice with cultural roots from Africa). Scholars like Zambakari have labored to unlearn imperialist concepts on the basis of what people know about conditions of forced migration *because of what they have learned while holding up under them*. In light of her participatory action research in South Sudan, Tarnjeet Kaur Kang insists on the asset-based assumption that people charting lives under forced migration are dynamic and mobile, rather than primarily in need or compromised. Zambakari applies the idea of dynamism and mobility to failed nation-building efforts in South Sudan: "the colonial state penalizes those that are most dynamic and brand them as aliens, non-indigenous, or foreigners" ("South Sudan" 106). Thus, in the next section of this paper, I employ concepts of Herbert Hermans and Sara McKinnon who, though not expressly decolonial in orientation, have articulated practices and theories that defy entrenched norms in order to do justice to what they've learned from people navigating harsh contemporary realities.

- **regularly renegotiating conditions of collaboration: "Intu lisa maya?"** *Are we still in this together?* "Intu lisa maya?" is an expression that members of the South Sudanese community in Phoenix often say while testing the terms under negotiation for a given collaboration. As a case in point, recall the vote the male leader called for in textbox 2. In calling for that vote, he led with the question, "Intu lisa maya?" To his question—*Are we still in this together?*—the eleven women made their answer clear: *No, not on these terms.* Then, with marked attention to their own purposes, just as soon as the meeting had adjourned, members of the women's leadership council began informally networking with others in the room—extending invitations for engagement to Jen, me, and the men who had called the meeting. They worked to venture something that might become a better alternative to what existed. After all, they suggested, our lives are still bound up in one another's. Julia's idea for talking groups was born, in part, from this renegotiation. And by extension, the talking group at Ruth's hair salon persists as an unfolding response to renegotiated conditions for collaboration.

- **heeding epistemic freedom's criticality, including the innate ability to know in one's bones what injustice feels like and to draw on experience—one's own and others'—as sources of insight for articulating what goes down in incidents of injustice and what might be done in response to them.** "Epistemic freedom," writes Ndlovu-Gatsheni, is "[f]undamentally, the recognition that all human beings were born into valid and legitimate knowledge systems" (Mudimbme qtd. in Ndlovu-Gatsheni 887). Julia's idea for the talking groups—that they would be multilingual and not require a particular threshold of schooling—reflects this premise. Cognitive justice foremost protects epistemic freedom by "recogni[zing] the different ways of knowing by which diverse people across the human globe make sense of the world and provide meaning to their existence" (887).

It's the next turn in Ndlovu-Gatsheni's argument that gets particularly challenging. Colonizing frameworks have perpetuated ideas—the very tools we use to think with—that would deracinate people from concepts that would do justice to their experiences. This deracination protractedly perpetrates cognitive injustice. Consequently, people have to be able to invent together new conceptual tools for the deeply critical, decolonizing work that Ndlovu-Gatsheni argues is most necessary. He writes: "[I]f we are to do anything about our individual and collective being today, then we have to coldly and consciously look at what imperialism has been doing to us and to our view of ourselves in the universe" (888). Over the course of "Cognitive Empire," Ndlovu-Gatsheni argues that decolonial practices need to construct means capable of this critical work; that such efforts are ontological as well as epistemic; and the work is within grasp in non-elitist, socially embedded locales. The rhythm of the talking group enacts one version of such activity. As textboxes 1 and 3 indicate, during the talking group, women share charged experiences navigating institutional systems. Then in taking up one another's concerns, they render details from similar accounts as resources that might help create more options. Critical race theorist Zeus Leonardo offers an analytical practice for carrying out this work—a practice that matches the patterned treatments of Black bodies across systems.[5]

- **making matters material**: Ndlovu-Gatsheni lauds the decolonizing contributions of Africa's premier knowledge-building academic organization: the Council for the Development of Social Science Research in Africa (CODESRIA). He credits the organization with having "produced some of the most groundbreaking research that directly confronted Eurocentrism" and with having "published some of the most influential works on the university in Africa and politics of knowledge production" (893). This study takes its cue from CODESRIA's charter which prioritizes "*policy*-oriented research ... *relevant* to the *demands* of the *African people*" (Article 4; emphasis added). In this spirit, albeit modestly, this study is committed to the material conditions of emergent publics (Long and Clifton). It is on this basis that this study strives not only to make legible how women leverage thanduk to build material infrastructure relevant to the demands of their lives, but also to listen for policy implications.

As practiced at the salon, thanduk undertakes two significant and timely demands: engaging the cultural differences that indirect rule has weaponized as the basis for interethnic violence; and negotiating the moral code that neoliberal economics promotes as the basis for a good citizen. Importantly, these tasks are undertaken in the service of the group's individual and collective thriving.

III. The Vibrancy of Thanduk

As the talking group attests, thanduk at once engages what the women know about the particular life circumstances they are navigating, and simultaneously provides resources to sustain the women who practice it within a network of mutual commitment.

Cultural Explanations of Thanduk

The women's explanations of thanduk are rooted in an interdependent orientation toward the land and animals, particularly cattle. The practice safeguards against other exigences coming along and claiming the capital one had intended to save, as the following analogy told for my benefit, illustrates. Nyayoi explained:

If you are someone who always tries to sell your cow and you have five cows and one of your cows has a baby, you say, *I take this and sell it and take the money and buy this and this and this.* [If you do that] you waste the cow['s potential value], by keep selling them or killing a cow. Soon all five of the cows are done. See? You can't really make your stuff to grow. Sometime people say, I used to have a lot but they all gone because I can't keep myself away from them. So I say, *this cow, I am going to give it to my neighbor. You can use the milk, just don't kill my cow. But all the benefits that come from that cow, you keep them. But it's my cow. Don't kill no babies.* So maybe by the time you bring back that cow, maybe it's had five babies or four babies. You see that? So you see, you really want to know who it is that you combine yourself with.

Nyayoi ties the practice of thanduk to an interdependent cultural practice curtailed by tribal conflict in South Sudan. Below, she explains this tradition to me in relation to her family's approach to farming, an approach that involved moving frequently in search of land to farm.

> **Nyayoi:** Let's say I move back to Tempe, maybe you have a lot of land around you. If I move there as your guest and ask if I can live here, you say, "Yeah, sure, you know what! You want this area? On this side? Take that land!" And then I build within [gestures boundaries].
>
> **Ellie:** And then, say, once your parents moved, another family could come and negotiate that?
>
> **Nyayoi:** Yeah! If someone wants to build their home where we used to stay, they can, too.
>
> **Ellie:** How come people are willing to do that? Because wouldn't the farmer say, "I want that land, too"? "I wanna be able to farm both the lands"?
>
> **Nyayoi:** Because, you know, in South Sudan, land is free. It's free and it's big. If someone wants this one so bad, I say, "Okay. We're not going to fight." You know? I thought it's mine, but if you really want it so bad, you take it! I'll move over there. Before it was easy, but I don't know what it's like now. People are so rude, so mean. Back in the day, every location my family moved, they don't buy.
>
> **Ellie:** That house where your mom lived —
>
> **Nyayoi:** Still exist? Nah, these days it's a forest. People move out, that area nobody. Just forest, even when you pass by in a boat on the sea. It's too scary, it's like forest. Because of this tribal fighting and stuff, they kill and they kill and they kill until you just leave the area. Nobody there. People move to the opening areas. Because of the war, everybody move and nobody build. (TGM 9/11/2021)

The inclination to share land that Nyayoi experienced as a child has been documented in scholarship (Mamdani; Zambakari "South Sudan"). I want to be careful not to minimize the complex and bloody histories of the broader Nuba Mountains region— histories of violence spanning from pre-colonial to colonial and post-colonial eras.

But all the more remarkable, then, that for thousands of years, the pastoralist and nomadic people found ways to live on and share the land and its resources.

Thanduk Wrangles Indirect Rule & Neoliberal Economics

What would count as evidence that thanduk resists the racialized politics of indirect rule and the lure of neoliberal economics? When intertribal conflict runs so deep, when neoliberal economics is so pervasive, how could it be claimed that the women find ways to build relationships and create outcomes that matter to them on other terms? These are questions that the talking group itself takes up.

Thanduk Thwarts the Racialized Politics of Indirect Rule

Working relationships at the hair salon transpire in relation to the interethnic politics that the women otherwise navigate as members of their communities. In Sudan in the 1930s and 40s, missionaries translated the bible into tribal languages in attempt to keep the Muslim faith from spreading below the tenth parallel. Now in Phoenix, community events like weekly religious services, weddings and funerals, and youth events continue to organize community members along the lines of these distinctive linguistic and religious affiliations. And members sometimes express deep animosity along these fault lines. Yet through thanduk, the women's relationships with one another reject the racialized us-them binary of indirect rule that has framed cultural differences as political disaffiliations worth killing for and dying over (Mamdani 197).

Significant, then, is the fact that neither the shop in general nor thanduk in particular is an enclave for a particular ethnic group. The braiders at Ruth's shop are mostly Nuer women, but Dinka and Arab women work there, too. From time to time, men have worked there, as well, including a white multiethnic American, as well as a newcomer from Mexico whom Ruth taught to braid hair. A new braider at Ruth's salon doesn't automatically get (nor is ever obligated) to practice thanduk with others at the salon. Invitations are issued when the number of participants falls below ten, most often when someone moves away or stops working. Then another woman—most often another braider from the shop, but not necessarily— is invited to join. (Most often another braider, that is, because to play ball you need the cash that a job like braiding can supply.) Senior members in the thanduk circle do not issue an invitation on the basis of the woman's ethnicity. Rather, they issue an invitation on the basis of a candidate's reputation: that she is known to be both trustworthy and good for it—good for, that is, her bi-weekly contributions to the pot.

Even so, it's impossible for the salon to operate outside of the histories of conflict—between Sudan and South Sudan, as well as between the Nuer and Dinka—that have produced the women as refugees. As a braider and member of the talking group named Akech put it recently during a talking group session: "Here in Phoenix ... I know some people acting weird about being Nuer or being Dinka, but to me, here in America we're here for different reason." Ruth then took the floor to respond that, as the shop owner, she'd rather lose a trusted braider than make the shop a place where interethnic tensions drive her business decisions. She recounted a situation a few months earlier: two of her braiders who were Nuer had asked her to stop employing a Dinka woman because some in Phoenix's Nuer community had issues with her family. Ruth recounted having told them, "Whatever is going on, I don't want to be in between. All I can say is if you don't like to see them, maybe you decide for yourself" (TGM 9/25/2021). In the end, the two Nuer women decided to put up with intertribal tensions that elsewhere fuel what would be perceived as intolerable animosity. The economic benefits of working at Ruth's shop prevailed, namely, the chance to earn cash braiding hair for a few hours between shifts at other jobs. The opportunity to earn cash —and the possibility of participating in thanduk—encouraged the Nuer women to position themselves differently in relation to a Dinka woman than they previously had thought possible.

Although the women participating in thanduk have no formal training in facilitating dialogue across difference, the talking group is a site of such collaborative theorizing. When used to shine light underneath the women's theorizing, Hermans's Dialogic Self Theory (DST) highlights key insights. Developed as part of the Netherlands' efforts to reckon with its colonial premise, DST is a psychological theory that integrates the ideas of *dialogue* and *multiple positions of the self* to account for "the intense interplay between power relations in the society at large and dominant relations in the 'mini-society' of the self" (Hermans, "Increasing Multiplicity" 4). Grounded in the Arjun Appadurai's critique of colonial rule and Mikhail Bakhtin's idea of the dialogic imagination, DST fosters people's capacities to build liberatory internal (psychological) and external (social) "coalitions" across difference ("Self" 134). I-positions are the most basic unit of the self in DST.

The talking group participants are keenly aware of how political tactics distort what they know experientially to be true about the relational nature of their cultural differences. DST can illuminate nuances of their insights. DST critiques the idea of a more or less singular, fixed and authentic self as reified in traditional psychology; so, too, the women in the talking group. This idea foments animosity toward others—rationalizing "cultural dichotomies [that] are dividing people instead of relating them" (Hermans and Kempen 1115). The women reject the binary colonial logic that, in Sudan, pitted Arabs against Africans, Christians against Arabs, and then Nuer against Dinka. DST can illuminate the means by which the women do so. To be clear, cultural dichotomies perpetuate an Insider-versus-Outside/Us-versus-Them meta-narratives that the women at the salon, like others in South Sudanese kinship networks, navigate in their daily lives. Some of the most persistent include North/South, Arab/Christian, Nuer/Dinka, and Men/Women. Yet conversations in the talking group reveal a more complex reality. In a recent talking group discussion, Nyayoi referenced her own heritage as she critiqued ways in which politicians in South Sudan fuel interethnic conflict. She began: "Like me, for example, Nyayoi, I have Dinka blood in my body, too, you know? I'm a Nuer woman, and I'm a Nuer, Nueramerga, I'm a Nuer lady. But I'm not gonna hate Dinka people because they Dinka, because I'm half Dinka." Then she rejected the very premise of conflict predicated on tribal differences: "Even if I'm not half Dinka, I'm fully Nuer, I will not hate Dinka people because they Dinka." Her argument concluded with her critique of the national debate in South Sudan: "But whatever politicians do in Africa, that crazy politics" (TGM 9/25/2021).

The talking group members also value the capacity to flex among multiple vantage points (or I-positions) as an asset for building relationships across differences, an important thesis for DST, as well. In their discussions, the women bear witness to identities—both their own and those of others—more varied and dynamic than those they inherited through Sudanese tribal conflict. These identities afford different resources for building connections with others. The capacity to flex across such positions is an asset for building relationships in Phoenix's refugee community. For instance, a talking group member named Akech channeled a dialogical spirit of self when accounting for a colleague's ethnicity: "Because sometimes [she and her family] say they're Dinka Belanda—like Dinka, but another group. And then sometimes they say they Bari, they say they Zande," depending on who they're talking to, the grounds on which the two conversation partners might forge a point of connection. But, Nyayoi chimed in, this dialogical orientation is not naive. She teased that as a world-wise parent, she had other I-positions available to her than simply that of her Nuer ethnicity: "Like, I have kids, I have a daughter, if my daughter comes home with a Dinka boy, I'm not going to hate that boy because he's Dinka. I'm gonna hate him for whoever he is [laughter], whatever he do, for his personality. Not because he's Dinka. You know?" In characteristic form, Nyayoi mobilized humor as a resource for positioning herself in relation to others in ways that refuse the terms of interethnic conflict (TGM 9/25/2021).

Indirect rule exploited the importance of relationships in South Sudanese culture to weaponize cultural differences. By politicizing tribal affiliations, this logic restricted what a cultural affiliation even means, making this position foremost an us-vs.-them binary—something to defend at all costs and at the expense of other ways of relating. In contrast, the women in the talking group are impatient with us-vs.-them positioning for the ways it restricts how they know to forge connections and build networks. In *The Handbook of Dialogical Self Theory and Psychotherapy: Bridging Psychotherapeutic and Cultural Traditions*, Hermans and colleagues demonstrate that DST supports culturally sustaining, transpersonal healing through which people connect with relational as well as spiritual resources beyond the self. All the more significant, then, that in *Culture, Trauma and Transpersonal Psychology: A Contemporary Study of South Sudanese*, South Sudanese psychologist John Kuek commends approaches to trauma-recovery that encourage access to transpersonal resources, foremost, relational support. Running in and across DST, Kuek's work, and the talking group, this trans/polyvocal premise affords the individual expressive latitude and rhetorical resources for building relationships across differences. Simultaneously, the dynamism of this stance grants that others, likewise, have their own arrays of cultural, experiential resources for building relationships across differences. As Kuek's work has shown, building coalitions in and across these networks has nurtured mutual healing.

Thanduk Negotiates the Neoliberal Moral Code

Additionally, Thanduk negotiates the prevailing moral code that suggests moral goodness is a prerequisite for actions independent of state approval—a strength of character earned through economic self-sufficiency.

On the one hand, for thanduk to translate cross-culturally to Phoenix, the shop's reputation as a small business needs to reinforce the women's moral reputations as relative newcomers to the US who are "in the ... process of becoming a good, successful, moral, and respectable citizen" (Stanley par. 6). Thanduk relies on the legitimacy of Ruth's shop in the eyes of the state. The practice works among the braiders in large part because customers pay in cash. From each appointment, as shopkeeper, Ruth keeps 40 percent and reports that as taxable income. From that appointment, the braider, then, keeps the remaining 60 percent. At the same time, the dynamics of the shop are interpolated with the racial politics of the US that foment hostile race relations with customers and incite extortion, death threats on social media, and even a recent lawsuit. Ruth told the group that what she finds most difficult as a small business owner are "the dangerous attitudes of the customers" (TGS 8/28/2021). Ruth recounted death threats on Facebook when the shop was not able to accommodate a customer's schedule on demand and a recent lawsuit that had caused her tremendous stress (TGS 8/28/2021). Describing the plaintiff's allegation that a braider had caused her hair to fall out, Ruth made clear that what mattered to the judge was that her business operated under state licensure: "The judge see it as the plaintiff was just trying to take advantage of our business, and our business not illegal because I have a state business license and what I was doing was not illegal. I don't do no chemicals that can harm her hair or pull her hair away from her head. I use a simple grease which is not a chemical" (TGS 8/28/2021). As a business person, Ruth knows it is important for the shop to run "above board" to protect against exploitative tactics. When taken to court, the judge vouched for the shop because its license is up to date.

At the same time, thanduk rejects the morality code that grants the state jurisdiction over the women's finances. Thanduk's material capacity to reliably and regularly collect and circulate $3000 has to be illegible to the state. The premise here is relatively simple. As mentioned earlier, even families in which male heads of household have advanced degrees, they typically work in low-paying human-sector positions that qualify the family for financial state support. With financial assistance comes the scrutiny of the state regarding a family's financial affairs. Thanduk refuses the neoliberal premise that until entirely self-sufficient, the state has the right—the prerogative—to surveil all of your finances. At a recent talking group session, Nyayoi explained the basis of the $300 in cash that the women contribute to the pot: "Since it's cash money, it really doesn't bother your welfare case." The scrutiny is palpable. She continued: "You have your job that your bank knows about for your house, that your welfare officer knows for your case, but the money you have here, nobody know, only you (TGS 8/28/2021)." Thanduk is the women's only means for accessing significant capital that is not surveilled and already spoken for in a system that urges them to hustle harder, all while at the same time making it clear that they can never hustle hard enough to earn the self-sufficiency required to get the state off their back.

Regarding thanduk's particular relation to the state's regulatory purview, the theorizing of McKinnon is helpful. In "Unsettling Resettlement: Problematizing 'Lost Boys of Sudan' Resettlement and Identity," she offers an account of the rhetorical acumen with which refugees refuse subjecting their moral make up to the scrutiny of the state. McKinnon's account cites Aihwa Ong's *Buddha Is Hiding: Refugees, Citizenship, the New America*. She writes:

[R]egulating techniques used by the state to form refugees into proper-subjects rarely work out as planned. However, refugees will make the resources work, for "subjects interpret and act in ways that undo systems of classification (cultural, ethnic, moral), refuse different kinds of objectives (involving needs, desires, behavior), and thwart rules of surveillance and punishment" (p. 17). (411)

The hypocrisies of resettlement discourse are not lost on institutional representatives. To address them, analysts have called for new legal categories for classifying the deserving refugee (Shiff); for community-based intersectionalist partnerships (Veronis); for new approaches to long-term integration strategies (Frazier and Van Riemsdijk); and for accessible public spaces capable of creating positive emotional attachments (Wood et al.). In the meantime, thanduk is an intervention the women have devised for themselves, on their own terms, on their own time.

The practice of thanduk defies victim narratives even as it refuses familiar edicts that cast economic self-sufficiency as an individual, moral matter. Thanduk exposes the fact that edicts to try harder, start earlier, or plan ahead better are insufficient for securing the financial independence required to be a good and moral citizen in the eyes of the state. Rather than indicating that moral shortcomings are to blame for the challenges of resettlement, the practice of thanduk operates within the heat, sprawl, and economic disparities of daily life in Phoenix. Thanduk is a material response to the empirical reality that the neoliberal promise of mobility can't be trusted.

As practiced at the salon, thanduk affords practitioners material means for creating some sort of traction under conditions that otherwise make such traction mightily elusive—as the life experiences documented in textboxes 1-3 attest. Here, Erevelles's materialist feminism is instructive, concerned as it is with material outcomes affecting people's lives. She promotes a version of citizenship that includes "access to the social and material resources necessary for the achievement of both individual and communitarian purposes and plans" (170). The examples that follow dramatize, respectively, what access and mobility can mean via the resources materialized through thanduk.

Thanduk and the Matter of Access

In this first example, thanduk provided access to a state of being outside "perpetual transition" (McKinnon 398)—a sort of material and symbolic traction where one's expertise and capacity to make choices on the basis of that expertise is recognized and respected. Through thanduk, Nyayoi's expertise as a braider earned respect from people positioned to be her superiors in whose hands her market value would otherwise lie.

With money set aside through thanduk, Nyayoi paid tuition for cosmetology school. At a recent talking group session, she narrated what this tuition made accessible to her. On the one hand, paying tuition is required to earn the licensure needed to expand her repertoire from braiding hair to other, including more lucrative offerings such as cutting, coloring and straightening hair. At this point in time, Nyayoi has completed all necessary coursework but has yet to take the final exam. So, over time, thanduk afforded the means—the cash for tuition—by which she will access those credentials and the potential for this expanded repertoire of professional practice. Meanwhile, she accessed an experience that, as she told it, she valued for its capacity to set the record straight with other people positioned to be her superiors: the teachers at the cosmetology school.

A course module made visible to others that she has expertise—to be clear, precisely the *professional* expertise that she was paying to have someone teach her, the very thing tuition promised to help her accrue. This experience bore witness to know-how that the others desired, know-how that Nyayoi had developed independent of the school, outside any coursework, and that exceeded the teachers' own skill level.

Nyayoi ended up teaching the braiding modules in the class she was taking for her cosmetology license. Explaining the circumstances to the talking group, she said:

When it came time for the braiding module, they tell us, "You have to do this kind of braid and this kind of braid. And when the teacher explained it, she just knew how to explain it from what was on the paper. The teacher knew how to say what was on the paper. But not how to do it actually when she tried it. But when I do mine the way she said it on the paper, mine came out perfectly good and they all see.

"Oh, my god. How do you do it?" [Others in class ask.]

I say, "I am a braider. I braid hair for a living."

"Really?"

I say, "Yes."

And they ask me, "Can you do this kind of braid and that kind of braid?

And I say, "Yes." And I show them. (TGS 10/23/2021)

On the basis of the instruction she then provided her classmates and teachers, administrators at the beauty school began recruiting Nyayoi to join the staff as a teacher.

As Nyayoi recounted the recruitment effort, she emphasized the condition that, to her mind, is most salient. In order to teach at the school, Nyayoi would have to pursue even more credentials. But in that she has made progress—has all but earned licensure necessary to be a fully credentialed hair stylist—it all feels within reach. No, whether she can secure those credentials is not the contingency she names that matters. The contingency that matters is whether she will take them up on their offer. Whether or not to do so is her choice.

"They told me last time. When I finish my papers, like when I have my state [cosmetology] license, *if* I like, *it's my choice*. They tell me, '*If you like* [gives words extra emphasis] you could go back to school again and do 500 hours and then you could become a teacher here.' And they would pay me." (TGS 10/23/2021)

On the one hand, this wager extends the state of perpetual transition: *Go back to school, put in 500 more hours of practice. Only/then you can have what we hold out as a promise.* As Nyayoi recounts the experience, that's an old story, a familiar jag. Nothing new there. What is new, what is refreshing, is that someone positioned as her superior would grant that whether to pursue that wager is not self-evident, not an obligation. But rather her choice.

Thanduk and the Matter of Mobility

In this second example, thanduk modulates urban sprawl that exacerbates the problem of resettlement as a state of "perpetual transition" (McKinnon 397). While Nyayoi used her thanduk funds for tuition, a braider named Mia used her thanduk for a car—a vehicle for navigating restrictive gender politics at home and the mobility required to practice her English with other people. Nyayoi's and Mia's decisions are just two examples from the talking group of diverse embodiments—different ways of building infrastructure—for navigating contingencies with limited resources. Together with the analogy of a neighbor safeguarding one's cow, the explication below borrows from Dolmage's theory of movement to make visible what Mia achieves through thanduk. Mia's ability to get a car with thanduk is one of hundreds of possible—albeit constrained—diverse embodiments for movement that the braiders make available to themselves by sharing resources.

Here in the Phoenix metropolitan area, public transportation is a viable day-to-day option for members of refugee communities relocated downtown. But by the time the women featured in this study settled in Phoenix, a relocation strategy dispersed members of the same refugee community in the name of cultural integration. If you haven't been to Phoenix, it can be hard to imagine just how vast the sprawl of the metropolitan area is—and, by extension, how debilitating it is for a community to be spread out like this. With housing prices downtown skyrocketing, even families who resettled in the area decades ago turn to the outskirts of the metropolitan area for housing. But here they must provide their own transportation to accomplish daily demands.

It's no wonder then that women often use thanduk to purchase used cars. Consider Mia's situation. After a car accident, her husband sold the title of the car out from under her in an insurance-fraud scheme. She was able to buy herself another car because of the $8000 she had saved through thanduk. Important to what thanduk can teach about mobility, it's not the car-as-object that's particularly meaningful here, but what the car allows Mia *to do*. As she explained during the talking group, without a car of her own, she would have been dependent on her husband to go anywhere—with exponentially limiting effects: on her capacity to earn her own money, to practice English, to continue her own education and to develop her own self-advocacy skills from what she learns from the other women at the shop.

The value of thanduk could be interpreted this way: pressures of daily life will likely compel you to give in to or indulge the I-position that would have you liquidate your assets—unless you have the benefit of trusted advocates who can nurture an alternative I-position for you by safeguarding those assets as they grow. Consider this self-other relationality alongside Dolmage's contention that mobility is a shared responsibility, not primarily a private matter. Mia's circumstances highlight the braiders' familiarity with contingencies. Thanduk anticipates that things will happen outside one's control—the catch is, you just can't predict what precisely they'll be. In Mia's case, these contingencies were the car accident followed by her husband's financial shenanigans that left her without a car. That is, in the very moment she needed them but couldn't have predicted, Mia had the means to cope with the circumstances because of the $8000 she had put away in savings from three consecutive turns at thanduk. The women in the thanduk circle help produce and safeguard one another's assets so they're available in the case of an emergency. Just as Mia has benefitted from the women in the circle safeguarding her savings, so, too, she has safeguarded not only her own but also the savings of the other women.

The gender politics that Mia navigates at home are restrictive. Resources earned at the salon and put aside through thanduk have expanded her options when those politics threatened to restrict her movement. A while back, Nyayoi and Mia recalled how Mia first came to the salon: Nyayoi said that Mia was among people who have come to the salon "to learn a skill for making money, too. Some of the women here didn't know how to do hair before. And I teach them." Nyayoi explained her response to Mia's request for lessons. About the hair braiding lessons specifically, Nyayoi explained why she went to the effort to teach Mia: "When somebody wants something really bad and you know it, you help her, too. By this world, it [charting a life] is by helping. Somebody do that to me; and I have to do it to other people if I have the kind of things they need. That's the life" (TGS 7/15/2017).

At a recent talking group session, Mia explained the value of having a car in terms of her capacity to navigate contingencies—an insight resonant with the kairotic quality of movement on the red helical ramp at the BART station in Berkeley, CA. Sure, she used it to earn a living. But the story she narrated was about another journey, another destination. She talked about the English she has learned because she has been able to get herself to the salon to be in the company of braiders—activity she would have been severed from without a car. Mia credited her enrollment in language classes to working at the salon. "I go to English classes because of being here. Since Ruth opened this shop, I've been working every Saturday with her. This is where I first learned English. When I started, I didn't say nothing. By being here, I got interested in learning, in taking classes. Now I don't go to sleep without reading." Ruth added affirmatively: "She's very good. She's learning" (TGS 10/23/21).

What Mia is learning at the shop increases her discursive mobility—her rhetorical capacity to navigate communicative encounters elsewhere. Mia urged Ruth to translate from Nuer to English:

When they [women like Mia] see me [Ruth] going here, they see me doing my own thing by myself. When I take my kids to the hospital, Biel doesn't go with me. And the others, when they go, their husbands go, too, to translate everything. And if something happens at their house, they can't take care of it. They have to wait for their husbands to do it. You see? And that's hard. And I do everything by my own. So they see it. They want to be like that. (TGS 10/23/21)

As this exchange attests, the rhetorical know-how required for Ruth, then Mia, to navigate institutional encounters, such as medical appointments, is itself a tool—one that becomes infrastructure when put to use. The process of acquiring it is communal, iterative and slow going. Thanduk coordinates the embodied cooperation it takes to produce movement within the means available at any given moment in time. Thanduk celebrates the collaborative and responsive feat of inventing traction—the *when* and the *who* as well as the *what*—required to compose mobility in sites of contingency.

Extending such networks transnationally, thanduk also funds reminders to families in relocation centers and camps that prove they aren't forgotten, especially, as Erevelles would predict, in providing access to medical care and groceries. In this way, thanduk networks an infrastructure of reciprocity that extends beyond the salon or even Phoenix. And as in the case where a large sum of money went to an airplane ticket for Nyayoi's daughter, thanduk instantiates the last thread of hope that elders "back in Africa" may be available and willing to take in and provide respite, inspiration and existential traction for troubled and justifiably angry South-Sudan-American teens.

Conclusion: A Thanduk-Based Heuristic

The limitations of retrofitting aren't exclusive to physical architecture. They extend to other domains of public life, as well. Furthermore, retrofitting won't ever be sufficient to rectify systemic injustice. In their bones, the women in the talking group know this. They know that the challenges each of them is navigating are particular and, thus, poorly suited to retrofitting. Yet that's just the beginning of the story. In thanduk, they are each theorizing this individual experience with people who are experiencing different individual experiences navigating the same systems. So configured, thanduk inspires the question: *How might community-university partnerships attend to individuals' embodied knowing, on the one hand, and methods of community organizing, on the other, in ways that are deliberately synergistic?* In the service of this big question follow several others, including:

Conditions of scarcity may leverage difference to fuel antagonisms. *If he wants this X, surely, then, I must have X, too. But there's not enough of X to go around, so one of us will have to lose.* But thanduk reminds us that this premise might not be necessarily true. *Maybe what I need is actually something different.* In Sudan, colonialists made access to scarce resources contingent on one's affiliation with the ethnic group deemed the majority of a given region. Land sharing worked by an altogether different premise. "You know? I thought it's mine, but if you really want it so bad, you take it! I'll move over there." By implication, we might consider in our own partnerships, *have we possibly internalized binaries that have a hold over how we now know to relate to one another? Whose interests are those categories actually serving? How might we breathe life into the spaces between and among our different I-positions to build coalitions that would not have otherwise been imaginable?*

Through the decisions they make in the service of access and mobility, women prize movement in defiance of the specter of slow death. There's joy in helping one another find that traction. *I had a hand in you doing that and you doing that… and you that…and that!* There's also sweet relief in knowing a handful of other people are paying attention to what you know is good for yourself or what you hope might be respite for someone you care about, but that you can't bring about on your own—and more to the point—that you know you will be tempted to relinquish when more immediate exigences make demands on your time and money. By implication, we might consider in our own partnerships *how having one another's backs might extend to include nurturing the means people need to mediate the complex contours of their lives that they know best?*

Across the talking group, epistemic status is distributed to cultivate shared theorizing that informs what women do with the money they save through practicing thanduk together. By implication, we might consider in our own partnerships *how to access and distribute epistemic contributions as resources for shared and <u>consequential</u> theorizing where the particularities of what it takes to navigate unjust systems become grist for distributing the informed responsibility of creating more sustaining pathways?*
The world's retrofitted fixes are clearly not working for a lot of people. Thanduk ventures the question, *How could things be otherwise?* And it directs resources toward making it so.

Notes

1. My heartfelt gratitude to the participants of the talking group who have granted permission to share their knowledge for the purpose of this study. As a condition, pseudonyms are used throughout. I would also like to thank reviewers of a previous draft for their most generous and formative feedback. Pascale Jarvis and Jennifer Clifton have contributed heart and soul, as well. Thank you.

2. Sanduk—with an s—is the more typical spelling. In Nuer, the "th" letter combination makes the sound of "s" in English. Variations of this kind of rotary credit or savings association are thought to be "indigenously African, and can be traced back to 1843, the date in which the practice is first mentioned in the Yoruba vocabulary" (Bonnett 40). Among the Sudanese, the use of the term *sanduk* reflects the spread of Islam and Arabic in the Sahel region of current day Sudan through military conquest and trade relations, spanning the 8th to 16th centuries. By using the Nuer spelling, the circle's leader, Nyayoi, invokes a cultural legacy—"setting something aside" that is distinct from the Arabic and now militarized connotations associated with the more typical translation of sanduk as box.

This study aligns with disability justice's proclamation that disability is not to be avoided; vulnerabilities are inherent to the human condition. It also pursues a second tack of disability justice: to address forces that produce disability as an intersectional phenomenon networked across markers of race, gender, sexuality, and class. For scholarship documenting the disabling consequences of normative institutional discourses, see Corker, Mairian, and Sally French, eds. *Disability Discourse*. Open UP,

1999; and Flower, Linda. "Going Public—in a Disabling Discourse." *The Public Work of Rhetoric*, edited by John Ackerman and David Coogan. U of South Carolina P, 2013, pp. 137–56.

4. The first group of Sudanese refugees—those featured in McKinnon's study—were, in fact, relocated to a central location; the Lost Boys Center was centrally located on Van Buren Street, easily accessible by bus from most all the young men's apartment complexes. Similarly, the Somali community has been able to sustain a culturally sustaining day care in large part because when the Somali community was first relocated in Phoenix, families were relocated in proximity of one another which allowed them to design a successful, shared day-care. But in more recent years, changes in relocation practices, as well as the search for affordable housing, has dispersed the South Sudanese community to the outskirts of Phoenix's urban sprawl. This often means that families in the same extended kinship network may live fifteen to thirty miles (or more!) away from one another or any central location. It's one thing to navigate public transportation to travel that distance once a week for church, but another for day-to-day demands of work, school, the house and kids.

5. A *patterned treatment*, according to Leonardo, is an "enduring," or patterned, way of treating members of a social group (39). Patterned treatments (such as microaggressions or protocols such as stop and frisk) are carried out in real time, on actual mindbodies; they communicate experiential information (embodied know-how) about how domination and other abuses of power "go down" and what it feels like to be caught in the throes of such institutional violence. Tracing the dis-location of Black girls in mainstream US educational systems, Erevelles's chapter "Of Ghosts and Ghetto Politics" is an academic example engaging the analytical practice of matching patterned treatments.

Works Cited

Alkebulan, Adisa A. "The Spiritual and Philosophical Foundation for African Languages." *Journal of Black Studies*, vol. 44, no. 1, 2013, pp. 50-62.

Ardener, Shirley. "The Comparative Study of Rotating Credit Associations." *The Journal of the Royal Anthropological Institute of Great Britain and Ireland*, vol. 94, no. 2, 1964, pp. 201-29.

Arizona Department of Health Services. "Pathways to Wellness: An Innovative Approach to Refugee Behavioral Health." *Refugee Health*, no. 4, 2015, p. 1.

Asante, Molefi Kete. *Afrocentricity: The Theory of Social Change*. African American Images, 2003.

Berlant, Lauren Gail. *Cruel Optimism*. Duke UP, 2011.

Blandin, Venton. "Valley Groups Among Push to Get More People of Color Involved in Outdoor Activities." ABC15.com. 23 February 2022.

Bonnett, Aubrey Wendell. *Rotating Credit Associations Among Black West Indian Immigrants in Brooklyn: An Exploratory Study*. 1976. City University of New York, PhD dissertation.

Clifton, Jennifer. "Feminist Collaboratives and Intercultural Inquiry." *Feminist Teacher*, vol. 24, no. 2, 2014, pp. 110-37.

—. "Mastery, Failure and Community Outreach as a Stochastic Art. *Unsustainable: Re-Imagining Community Literacy, Public Writing, Service-Learning and the University*, edited by Jessica Restaino and Laurie JC Cella. Rowman & Littlefield Publishing Group, 2013, pp. 227-52.

CODESRIA Charter. June 2015. https://codesria.org.

Dolmage, Jay. "'Breathe Upon Us an Even Flame': Hephaestus, History, and the Body of Rhetoric," *Rhetoric Review*, 2006, vol. 25, no. 2, 119-40.

—. "From Steep Steps to Retrofit to Universal Design, from Collapse to Austerity: Neo-liberal Spaces of Disability." *Disability, Space, Architecture: A Reader*, edited by Jos Boys, Routledge, 2017, pp. 102-13.

—. "Mapping Composition: Inviting Disability in the Front Door." *Disability and the Teaching of Writing: A Critical Sourcebook*, edited by Cynthia Lewieck-Wilson and Brenda Jo Brueggeman, with Jay Dolmage. Bedford/St. Martin's, 2008, pp. 14–27.

Duggan, Lisa. *The Twilight of Equality? Neoliberalism, Cultural Politics and the Attack on Democracy*. Beacon P, 2003.

Erevelles, Nirmala. *Disability and Difference in Global Contexts: Enabling a Transformative Body Politic*. Palgrave Macmillan, 2016.

Frazier, Emily and Micheline van Riemsdijk, "When 'Self-Sufficiency' Is Not Sufficient: Refugee Integration Discourses of US Resettlement Actors and the Offer of Refuge. *Journal of Refugee Studies*, vol. 34, no. 3, 2021, pp. 3113-30.

Geertz, Clifford. "The Rotating Credit Association: A 'Middle Rung' in Development." *Economic Development and Cultural Change*, vol. 10, no. 3, 1962, pp. 241-63.

Hamlet, Janice. "Understanding African American Oratory: Manifestations of Nommo." *Afrocentric Visions: Studies in Culture and Communication*, edited by Janice Hamlet, Sage, 1998, pp. 89-105.

Hermans, Hubert J. M. "Dialogical Self Theory and the Increasing Multiplicity of I-Positions in a Globalizing Society: An Introduction." *New Directions for Child and Adolescent Development*, vol. 2012, no. 137, 2012, pp. 1–21.

—. "Self as a Society of I-Positions: A Dialogical Approach to Counseling." *Journal of Humanistic Counseling*, vol. 53, no. 2, 2014, pp. 134-59.

Hermans, Hubert J. M., and Harry J. G. Kempen. "Moving Cultures: The Perilous Problems of Cultural Dichotomies in a Globalizing Society." *The American Psychologist*, vol. 53, no. 10, 1998, pp. 1111-20.

Kang, Tarnjeet Kaur. *Community Self-Determination in South Sudan: A Return to the Subaltern*. 2018. University of Illinois at Urbana-Champaign, PhD dissertation.

Kells, Michelle Hall. "Writing Across Communities: Deliberation and the Discursive Possibilities of WAC." *Reflections: A Journal of Community Engaged Writing and Rhetoric*, vol. 6, no. 1, 2007, pp. 87-108.

Kerschbaum, Stephanie, et al. "Faculty Members, Accommodation and Access in Higher Education," *Profession*, 2013.

Kershaw, Terry. "Afrocentrism and the Afrocentric Method." *Afrocentric Visions: Studies in Culture and Communication*, edited by Janice Hamlet, Sage, 1998, pp. 27-44.

Kessi, Shose, et al. "Decolonizing African Studies." *Critical African Studies*, vol. 12, no. 3, 2020, pp. 271-82.

Konopka, Agnieszka, et al. *The Handbook of Dialogical Self Theory and Psychotherapy: Bridging Psychotherapeutic and Cultural Traditions*, Routledge, 2019.

Kuek, John. *Culture, Trauma and Transpersonal Psychology: A Contemporary Study of South Sudanese*. 2015. Sophia University, PhD dissertation.

Leonardo, Zeus. "The Color of Supremacy: Beyond the Discourse of 'White Privilege.'" *Critical Pedagogy and Race*, edited by Zeus Leonardo, Blackwell, 2005, pp. 37-52.

Long, Elenore and Jennifer Clifton. "The Commons-in-Practice as an Antidote to Statelessness" *Proceedings for the 15th CODESRIA General Assembly: Africa and the Crisis of Globalisation*, 2018.

Long, Elenore and Tarnjeet Kaur Kang. "Reconfiguring Public Life: Refugee Education as Joint Inquiry." *Refugee Education: Integration and Acceptance of Refugees in Mainstream Society. Emerald Publishing*, edited by Enakshi Sengupta and Patrick Blessinger, 65-79.

Long, Elenore, et al. "Fostering Inclusive Dialogue in Emergent Community-University Partnerships." *Crossing Borders: The Rhetoric of Lines Across America*, edited by Patricia Wojahn and Barbara Couture, Utah State UP, 2016, pp. 227-53.

Mamdani, Mahmood. *Neither Settler nor Native: The Making and Unmaking of Permanent Minorities*. Harvard UP, 2020.

McKinnon, Sara L. "Unsettling Resettlement: Problematizing 'Lost Boys of Sudan' Resettlement and Identity." *Western Journal of Communication*, vol. 72, no. 4, 2008, pp. 397-414.

Mudimbe, Valentin Yves. *The Idea of Africa*. Indiana UP, 1994.

Ndlovu-Gatsheni, Sabelo J. "The Cognitive Empire, Politics of Knowledge and African Intellectual Productions: Reflections on Struggles for Epistemic Freedom and Resurgence of Decolonisation in the Twenty-First Century," *Third World Quarterly*, 2021, vol. 42, no. 5, 882-901.

Ong, Aihwa. *Buddha is Hiding: Refugees, Citizenship, the New America*, U of California P, 2003.

Osondu, Iheanyi N. "Rotatory Credit Schemes: A Comparative Analysis of an African Traditional Economic Institution in Contemporary Africa and Its Diaspora." Ìrìnkèrindò, vol. 4, 2011, pp. 138-65.

Rodgers, Selena. "Womanism and Afrocentricity: Understanding the Intersection." *Journal of Human Behavior in the Social Environment*, vol. 27, 2017, pp. 1-2, 36-47.

"Ṣandūḳ." *Encyclopaedia of Islam, Second Edition, Glossary and Index of Terms*, Leiden, Koninklijke Brill NV, 2012.

Shiff, Talia. "Reconfiguring the Deserving Refugee: Cultural Categories of Worth and the Making of Refugee Policy." *Law & Society Review*, vol. 54, no.1, 2020, pp. 102-32.

Simmons, W. Michele. "Attending to the Epistemological Status of Public Life." Keynote. Association of Rhetoric and Writing Studies. Austin, TX. 9 November 2019.

—. "Participation and Power: Civic Discourse in Environmental Policy Decisions." *Participation and Power*. State U of New York, 2007.

Stark, Lindsay, et al. "SALaMA Study Protocol: a Mixed Methods Study to Explore Mental Health and Psychosocial Support for Conflict-Affected Youth in Detroit, Michigan." *BMC Public Health*, vol. 20, no. 1, 2020, pp. 20-38.

Stanley, Anna. "Introduction to Addressing the Indigenous-Immigration 'Parallax Gap.'" *Radical Journal of Geography: Antipode Online*. 18th June 2014.

Tutlam, Nhial T., et al. "Emotional and Behavioral Disorders among US-Born Children of South Sudanese Parents Resettled as Refugees." *Global Social Welfare*, 2022, np.

Veronis, Luisa. "Building Intersectoral Partnerships as Place-based Strategy for Immigrant and Refugee (Re)settlement." *The Canadian Geographer*, vol. 63, no. 3, 2019, pp. 391-404.

White, Eric Charles. *Kaironomia: On the Will-To-Invent*, Cornell UP, 1987.

Wood, Patricia Burke, et al. "The Emotional City: Refugee Settlement and Neoliberal Urbanism," *Journal of International Migration and Integration*, vol. 13, 2011, pp. 21-37.

Zambakari, Christopher. "Challenges of Liberal Peace and Statebuilding in Divided Societies." Accord: Conflict Trends, vol. 4, 2016, pp. 18-24.

—. "South Sudan and the Nation-Building Project: Lessons and Challenges." *National Democratic Reforms in Africa*, edited by S. Adejumobi, Palgrave Macmillan, 2015, pp. 89-127.

Author Bio

Elenore Long is a professor of Writing, Rhetorics, and Literacies at Arizona State University. She examines and theorizes how displaced people engage with and respond to global, social, cultural and economic disruptions. Committed to supporting rhetorical dimensions of public life, she builds local partnerships with people whose access to the polity cannot be assumed or taken for granted. She has tested and refined a rhetorical model for intercultural inquiry across a range of participatory action research projects, including work with a Gambian American student organization, with the Nipmuck tribe, and with members of the South Sudanese diaspora in Phoenix, AZ. Most recently she published with Elizabeth Kimball and Jennifer Clifton *The Potentiality of Difference: Singular Rhythms of a Translational Humanities in Community Contexts* with Intermezzo.

Symposium

To Community with Care: Enacting Positive Barriers to Access as Good Relations

Cana Uluak Itchuaqiyaq, Caroline Gottschalk Druschke, Lauren Cagle, and Rachel Bloom-Pojar

Abstract

> This symposium builds from our discussions about communities, academia, activism, and access as four faculty members with different positionalities and perspectives to advocate for the protection of relations in the face of universities' demands for access to peoples, communities, and lands. In each of four individually authored reflections, we recount our experiences working with and being in community as part of our academic practice. We extend from work in disability studies to explain that while access is generally understood to be good, and often is, access can also be the precursor to exploitation. We argue that to mitigate that risk, we can take on a positive gatekeeping function as part of being in community with care.

Keywords

community, marginalization, access, relationships, ethics

Finding community is precious. Community nurtures our spirits and, often, inspires our work. What a community is–and how it is assembled, feels, and functions–are fluid and contextually based. For this article, we intentionally allow for space around defining community to instead focus on the act of *being in* community. To be in community means more than just "being part" or "being with," it also means being careful with the gift of connection brought about by community, whatever that means for you.

We are bringing together two conversations: one about community and one about access. Both are often presumed to be unquestionable goods; community and access are both positive, necessary parts of human thriving. In the context of disability justice particularly, access is a necessary condition for equity as well as vital to enabling disabled people to be in community. Even in that context, though, access is a contested concept, which Aimi Hamraie incisively highlights with their development of the idea of "access-knowledge," which foregrounds the fact that how access is defined and created is a process of knowledge-making. And importantly, that process is not immune to relations of power and effects of intersectional marginalization. Disability justice as a frame allows us to engage access critically, given the fact of access-knowledge. Outside of disability justice, thus, the concept of access risks misuse; it is all too easy to use the value of "access" to justify injustices, if access is treated as a universal and unexamined good. So, it is critical that, in our conversation about academics working in community, we question the role that appeals to access play.

As academics aiming to work in or with communities, we are perturbing a system, even when we already belong to that community ourselves. Our presence as academics changes the community and opens up multi-directional avenues between the community and the academy. The community is not a thing, a research subject, a closed system we can just study – it is a complex open system we affect and are—and should be—affected by in turn. And while access, defined as "the ability, right, or permission to approach, enter, speak with, or use; admittance" ("access"), is generally understood to be good, access can also be the precursor to exploitation. So, when we open up a community system, perhaps by giving others access to it, we put it at risk of exploitation. To mitigate that risk, we can take on a positive gatekeeping function.

This shared introduction places the work we describe in this piece, work we largely do independent of each other, but hardly alone. To open, we describe the central questions we each take up here, and which situate our work's complicated relation to access. This work largely consists of collaborations with non-university communities, which is most often legible within the academy as a form of research and co-production of knowledge. We explore the risks associated with these collaborations that marginalized members incur via providing access for outsiders to their communities. We consider what harm we cause in our community-based work, what power relations we create, unsettle, or reinscribe, and how we might co-create new stories about what it means to do this work in community.

This shared conversation came together through our Roundtable on Good Relations at the 2021 Conference on Community Writing. We assembled virtually there, along with Les Hutchinson Campos, to consider the ways that all of us are focused in our work on relations of all kinds and spend a large amount of time trying to maintain the "good." Our conversation was inspired in part by a question offered several years ago by Margaret Noodin, Associate Dean for Humanities at University of Wisconsin-Milwaukee, former Director of the Electa Quinney Institute for American Indian Education, and speaker and teacher of Anishinaabemowin: "Can you introduce yourself and include in your introduction the bodies of land and water that have given you life and are now protected and acknowledged by you?" We were moved as a group to reflect on that question and to add several related ones based on our work across technical communication, cultural rhetorics, community-based writing, and beyond: How can we, both we specifically and academics in general, make use of the cultural rhetorics pillars of story, relationality, constellation, and decolonization to foster good relations in our shared work? How can we co-create new stories about what it means to do this work in community? What risks associated with research and co-production of knowledge might marginalized members incur via providing access for outsiders to their communities? What harm might we—and *do* we—cause in our community-based work? How might community building with languages other than English help us deepen our understanding of good relations? How can we work against the impulse–and often the expectation–to "research"? (For an extremely partial list of works that inspired these questions, see: Edenfield, et al.; Hidalgo et al.; Itchuaqiyaq and Matheson; Powell et al; Rai and Druschke; Sparrow et al.; Tuck and Yang)

This collection of short responses works to address those questions, highlighting how we celebrate the relations that give us life in the context of community activism, community writing, and community-based scholarship. We share our work to join a call for scholar-teachers in community writing and rhetoric and composition to prioritize accountability towards our shared relations and we explicitly advocate for the protection of those relations in the face of universities' demands for access to peoples, communities, and lands. We see ourselves as scholar-activists concerned with these kinds of good relations—to peoples, to places, to ancestors, to histories, to plants and rivers, to organizations—in our work through, with, and in a variety of community settings: as Indigenous boundary spanner, as researcher in partnership with state environmental organizations, as new mother researching and working alongside promotores de salud, and as human-scholar working to support community-led initiatives in spite of fraught institutional relations.

No, I won't introduce you to my mama: Boundary Spanners, Access, and Accountability to Indigenous Communities

Cana Uluak Itchuaqiyaq

There exists an added pressure that Indigenous scholars and other marginalized scholars face as boundary spanners: marginalized scholars are asked to spend their personal social capital on other scholars' professional needs. I define boundary spanners as individuals who occupy both academic spaces and marginalized community spaces and who are called on to act as mediators between the two. This piece discusses my own navigation across these spaces and the nuances of relationship that I must recognize and respond to as an additional component of my professional and communal practice. I will also share about the difference between credibility and accountability and how that important distinction is often overlooked.

Briefly, boundary spanners link together systems of people, communities, institutions, and knowledges through their belonging to and expertise with both systems. As an Iñupiaq from an Alaska Native community in the Arctic, I have cultural and community expertise and connections from being part of that system. As a technical communication and rhetoric scholar and professor at an R1 institution, I have another set of expertise and connections from being part of that system. The boundary spanning I try to do is in the service of helping my Inuit community in Alaska with claiming and accessing institutional resources from academia.

The use of the word "claiming" above is intentional. My goal as a scholar is to help my people—Alaska Natives—who are severely underrepresented in academia claim the space they need to thrive in—or even just graduate—college. The term "Alaska Native" describes the Indigenous people who are part of the 229 federally recognized tribes in Alaska. For context, there are currently 574 federally recognized tribes in the United States. According to the Alaska Native Knowledge Network, the first known Alaska Native to earn a PhD was an Athabaskan named James Simpson in 1970 in Education. The first known Iñupiaq to earn a PhD was Paul A. Goodwin in 1979 in Physics. By the end of 2010—40 years after the first Alaska Native earned their doctorate—there were 62 PhDs. By 2015, the number had increased to 90. And, as of March 2022, the number has increased to 127 Alaska Native PhDs.

Of these 127 PhDs, there are 29 Iñupiat; I am #28.

Iñupiat homelands are located in the Alaskan Arctic and are roughly the same size as the state of New Mexico. I mention these statistics to make a specific point: while there are numerous Iñupiat who have research skills, there are just 29 who have that magic title—PhD—that can gain them entry as research faculty in academia. And, as I will discuss, that title means that others may consider these 29 scholars as entry points themselves to Iñupiat communities in the Arctic.

Iñupiaq PhD candidate Margaret Anamaq Rudolf's scholar bio states that "Boundary spanners facilitate research projects between Alaska Native communities and research institutes. Boundary spanning is one way to accomplish co-production of knowledge, which may be key in the context of working with Alaska Native communities" (Rudolf para 3). In terms of being a boundary spanner, I am called to use my personal social capital for my professional endeavors. This gets even more complicated when people—usually scholars with more institutional and disciplinary power than me who are seeking local Arctic partners in fulfillment of the increasing coproduction of knowledge requirements in grants—ask me to introduce them to people in my Alaska Native community.

Let's unpack what asking me to make introductions in my community means. What I'm really being asked to do is use my personal relationships that I've spent a lifetime building and rebuilding for their academic research needs. They are asking me to vouch for them to my people, my community, my friends, and my family. These askers think that their outsider-perspective research agenda is a big opportunity to my people and are shocked when I don't jump up enthusiastically, call my mama, and book them a spot on her couch. The funniest part is that sometimes I don't even know the people who are doing the asking. In other words, literal strangers are asking me to set them up with my family and community. That's some bullshit.

Why do they feel comfortable with this ask? Beyond entitlement, one reason may be a belief that our profession links us in a special way, and perhaps it does. However, let's not forget the ongoing history of harmful and extractive research practice in academia. I'm sorry, but I am not going to help rando scholars inflict their rando research agenda on my people. I will not risk the potential harm of that kind of set-up. Put another way, I'm an insider to my own Alaska Native community yet I am still very cautious about approaching my own people regarding my research. I don't assume that because I'm from the community that my people will welcome or need or want the research I might propose. In fact, it took me two years of careful discussions and small-scale collaborations to convince my big sister—literally someone who helped raise me and who knows that I come to my work with a good heart, meaning my motivations are centered in our people's wellbeing and needs rather than my own personal and professional ambitions—to partner with me on a project creating an online archive for Inuit users for our tribe. And, once we agreed on the project and the partnership, we then approached our tribal organization to make sure that the idea we had, an idea sparked from community needs, was welcome and wanted.

Respectful research in Indigenous communities requires that research problems and research questions related to Indigenous land and peoples must come from these communities themselves. As scholars, we need to respect community sovereignty and be humble enough to take the time to build local relationships and listen to local needs and wants and pivot our existing research and restructure new research questions to help fulfill those needs. For example, I am not a digital archivist but that's what my community needed. But as a scholar, a.k.a. a professional learner, I can learn about digital archives and combine it with what I know about technical communication and UX. Furthermore, as a boundary spanner, I can help enlist others with complementary skills to help. Keeping an open mind about what and how you might contribute to a community's self-determined needs is important. Sometimes conducting a research project isn't the right course of action for the community in fulfilling its needs. Sometimes a community might want to do the research themselves without you. Being in good relations with a community partner, such as acting with care for the community by supporting and upholding their needs and their boundaries, should not be conducted with a "what's in it for me" attitude. For generations, Indigenous communities have been promised that academic research in their communities would ultimately benefit their people. We have extended our trust and given access to our people and our lands even when the benefits to us were unclear or, sadly, unfulfilled. Perhaps it's time for academia to extend trust back to us, FFS.

This is where the distinction between credibility and accountability comes in. I might have the credibility to do research in my community based on my fancy degrees, position, and identity—but that credibility don't mean shit if I don't hold myself accountable to the self-determination and the sovereignty of my people. What does that accountability mean? It means caring more about the needs and safety of my community more than my own professional needs. Simply, it means putting my community first—in the position of power—when I choose to engage with them in my professional capacity. You see, as a scholar, I have a choice about what I study and therefore can, in essence, self-define my research goals. My community should also have these same choices. My goal as a scholar—to help my people—means that I am accountable to my people first, not my university. Affiliations to universities come and go, affiliations to communities should not.

When working with an Indigenous community, it's important to position accountability to that community and its needs as the primary factor of your work. Because Indigenous communities likely don't give a fuck about your title or your CV when it comes to your research ideas, they care about your heart.

Cultivating Soil, Cultivating Self

Lauren E. Cagle

I'll begin with a story about one of the most right things I have done in my life. When I moved to Kentucky in 2016 for my first faculty position, I was in an emotionally abusive marriage, smoking almost a pack a day and drinking far too much, to mute the abuse. And even as that was daily life, I was also excited to finally live somewhere that I could put down roots. I grew up a military brat, and lived in Boston and Memphis for college, Las Vegas for my master's, and Tampa for my PhD. I had never lived anywhere more than four years. I had no permanent home, no roots. Yet I study environmental rhetoric, so I was excited in an intellectual, abstract way about the idea of having a place, because I wondered how I could really understand environmental work if I wasn't attached to a place.

In Kentucky, my then-husband and I moved into a shotgun rental house at the far end of a gentrifying neighborhood. I thought it was perfect. I was going to learn how to garden, and I was going to plant things in the long narrow yard behind the house. I didn't know how to grow anything. I didn't even have houseplants. But it turned out that I couldn't plant things in that yard, anyway, because the ground was full of broken glass. I couldn't make up a better metaphor if I tried.

I remember asking friends online, what do you do with a yard full of broken glass? The answer was that you cover it in topsoil. And that seemed, and still seems, to me like an unideal situation. There's still broken glass down there. We cover up adulterated soil. Why do we not amend the soil, so that as it turns over, as plants' roots stretch down, as we dig for potatoes and carrots and beets, we don't cut our hands?

The non-metaphorical question about glass in the soil became moot six months later, when I walked out on that relationship and had a very sudden divorce. The house I moved into then was the first place I had ever lived by myself. The backyard was tiny, with a disused gravel path that led nowhere and a single rotting raised bed next to sparse grass. I was there for four years. I started gardening, first in pots, then in the ground itself, under the rotted raised bed I had broken up and cleared away. I grew butter lettuce and sparkler radishes and hollyhocks and red Russian kale and rainbow carrots and sunflowers and Bloomsdale long standing spinach and one single, perfect cauliflower. I started composting, and then added the finished compost to my garden. I learned how to hoe and till and amend and mulch and weed, sometimes from friends, sometimes from YouTube.

When I moved out of that house, a friend asked if I was bothered by having put so much effort into the soil, which I was now leaving behind. I had made a garden where there wasn't one. And my answer came immediately, though I did not know I knew this before I said it to her. I said, "There is so much soil all over this world. I have lived in so many places and walked on their soil. I have eaten food from infinitely more plots of land. So much soil has kept me alive and fed me during my life; the least I can do is not begrudge this soil whatever I've put into it."

Knowing and then saying that is one of the most right things I've ever done. Developing that relationship with the soil, that care for the soil I gardened with, that accountability to the soil that nourished me before I ever became a gardener, that was right.

It is not a relationship that sprang from nothing. I can trace the ways I was prepared to encounter soil in that way. Being in relation with the people I'm writing with in this symposium prepared me. Developing research collaborations with geologists and agricultural extension specialists and arborists prepared me. Reading work by Robin Wall Kimmerer and Kathleen E. Absolon Minogiizhigokwe and Zoe S. Todd prepared me. Learning from Earth First! activists and water protectors at Standing Rock and nuns from the Sisters of Loretto protesting the Bluegrass pipeline prepared me.

What we know, even what we don't know we know until we are asked to say it, rests on layers of what came before: the things we read, the images we see, and the relationships we cultivate.

Much of what I read, see, and cultivate comes from academia, including many of the roots of my relationship to soil. There's something oddly beautiful about an institution as fucked up as academia leading me to this relationship. That beauty is tempered by the fact that I can only enjoy it as much as I do because I have privileges that allow me to escape many of the harms academia causes. For me as an individual white, middle-class woman whose parents both have graduate degrees, academia is a place of welcome. I have access to academia, and to the resources it offers those invited in.

So, when I think of relations in relation to my academic work, I know that I am often in a position to offer academia's resources to those I am in relation with, including those academia may not have invited in. People often characterize my work as community-based participatory research, but most of my collaborations are with organizations, and not necessarily community organizations in the sense of community-led grassroots organizations, but largely with institutionally sanctioned organizations. For me, doing community-based work involves working with organically developed groups of people who coalesce around shared characteristics —e.g., living in the same neighborhood—or issues—e.g., being downstream of point-source pollution. Of course, these groups might organize into some kind of official structure; a neighborhood coalition focused on environmental justice might file the paperwork to create a non-profit, for example. So, the presence of an official structure or organization does not necessarily mean that there isn't a community there, but the organizations I work with are typically composed of professionals brought together by their expertise or work experience, not by shared personal characteristics or interests. And these organizations often hold institutional power—even when they're chronically underfunded. One of my closest collaborators, the Kentucky Geological Survey, is literally mandated to exist by law, which is about as institutionally sanctioned as it gets in the contemporary U.S.

Not intentionally, but through layer upon layer of relation-building and decision-making, I have aligned my research and teaching with these institutionally well-established organizations. That alignment is not necessarily a bad thing. There are benefits to having someone who has been taught to think about community and relations involved with these organizations; my role can become one of relationship-building between organizations and communities. In other words, when we think about the complex issues people face, the stakeholders frequently include official organizations such as my collaborators: the Kentucky State Division for Air Quality or the UK Recycling office, for example. These organizations have a service mission—and because of my personal research interests, I gravitate towards environmentally focused missions. But rather than beginning by working with a community or community group impacted by those organizations, I've found myself working with the organizations and then helping those organizations work with stakeholders outside, who may or may not self-identify as belonging to various communities.

But, through my engagement with my co-authors here, and the larger conversation we're pulling together about access, I have been thinking of late about how to articulate my role in these collaborations as an access point, whether that's to a community I've been asked to help scientists connect with, or perhaps to the resources of academia I'd like to put in the hands of under-resourced non-academics. More and more, I find myself telling my academic colleagues to not just go into communities, to not ask for non-academics' unpaid time, and to not assume that our research has value to the communities around us. Instead, I say, let us ask people in the communities where we want to do research what they need and want, and let us pay them—in funds or other reciprocal relations—for their time and expertise and goodwill. It has taken the layering of time and experience to be able to understand myself this way.

This understanding began for me in graduate school with courses on participatory action research and feminist research methods. But it is only in the building of relationships with official organizations trying to serve communities, and me trying to figure out my role and obligations in that process, that I have come to see how important access–granted or denied or negotiated–is to being in relation with people outside the academy. Ultimately, to even be in relation, I choose to give access to myself, and I ask for access to those with whom I am in relation. Being honest about the vulnerability that exchange demands allows me to take care with any responsibility for access I am given.

Whether or not I want the role, academia has made me a gatekeeper to its resources. I'm still working through what that means and all the ethical dimensions of it. But it's important to note that I haven't been made gatekeeper because I am somehow uniquely positioned to know best what others need. Rather, it's just because I happened to get this job as a tenure-track faculty member in rhetoric at an R1 university in the U.S. So, it's up to me to figure out how to take this imposed responsibility—gatekeeping the academy's resources—and manage it ethically in conversation with those I'm hoping to collaborate with on gaining them access to those resources.

My impulse when talking about good relations is to focus on how to have good relations with whomever you've already decided to work with. But as I foreground access in the relationships I build as an academic, I am taking a step back to ask a preceding question, with whom I want to have good relations. The relations we cultivate cultivate us in turn. I can open myself to that which will cultivate me well, and I can choose what and who that is. And I cannot cultivate good relations with others simply to produce something just for me or because I think I can cultivate them. I am the soil. I tend to the soil. I am not in control but what I do still matters.

Co-Creating Stories of Confianza

Rachel Bloom-Pojar

As I reflect on my community-engaged work from the past eleven years, I know that any successful partnerships I've had have been because my collaborators and I took the time to get to know each other as people and build confianza ("trust/confidence") together. As someone who works with Latinx communities but is not Latina, I am aware of how fragile that confianza can be, and I do my best to keep building on it by showing up and being mindful of how my actions are read in relation to the harm and objectification they may have experienced from other white academics. Researchers, especially white researchers, often aim to keep their personal lives and identities separate from the work they do. But when your work entails hearing stories about other people's lives, bodies, and relations, then you need to account for who you are in the emerging relationship and what you will do with access to the stories that anyone may share with you.

My commitments to community and orientation as a researcher today have been shaped by my relationships with a group of promotores de salud ("health promoters") at Planned Parenthood of Wisconsin (PPWI) and the director of their program, Maria Barker. Maria and I first connected in 2017 when I first moved to Milwaukee. We met once in fall 2017 to get to know each other and discuss the program, reconnected in winter 2018 at a retreat on Cultural Humility, and started regularly meeting and working together in 2019. Part of that work included co-designing an ethnographic project about reproductive justice, the promotores, and health communication. I met many of the promotores at four focus groups I held in October 2019. Those focus groups and my larger ethnographic project were designed with Maria's input about what she also hoped to learn from the research and how it might lead to practical findings that would highlight and support the work of the promotores. When I met many of the promotores during the focus groups, they trusted me to a certain extent because Maria trusted me, but many were also skeptical of what I would do with the things they shared, and they told me that they often didn't hear about what happened with the research they participated in. It would take a lot longer to build confianza beyond this initial interaction. Around that same time, I applied for a fellowship that would allow me to be in residence with the program for the following academic year. The need for this time became increasingly clear as my normal responsibilities at the university severely delayed my ability to work with the focus group transcripts or follow up with the promotores. I hated how this might reinforce the idea that I might be just like those other academics that they met with and never hear from again. Thankfully, I did receive that fellowship and our weekly interactions the following year helped alter the course of my research and our relationships as we got to know each other.

It's important to note that these promotores and my work with them have connections to community-based sex education and reproductive justice (SisterSong; Bloom-Pojar and Barker). So, when I write about confianza, I'm drawing from knowledge informed by the promotores and their experiences creating it within their communities. While the promotores create confianza to talk about lots of different health and community issues, the heart of their work includes the ability to create confianza and safe spaces for community members to talk about sexual and reproductive health. When individuals enter into confianza with the promotores, they often feel comfortable enough to start talking about culturally taboo topics like birth control, abortion, and sexuality, and many of them open up about experiences with unhealthy relationships, abuse, and/or wishing they better understood sex or personal bodily autonomy at a younger age.

I began my remote work with the promotores amid the first year of the Covid-19 pandemic. At this time, I was also navigating new aspects of my identity and reproductive health as a new mother. In May 2020, I delivered my first child and began parenthood amid the chaotic and uncertain start of a pandemic. Three months later, my father suddenly died. Three weeks after that, I began my fellowship work with PPWI. I had never had so many highs and lows happen within such a short period of time. I leaned into things that helped me feel connected and rooted to other people even when we couldn't be together in person. I experienced a chaotic merging of my personal and professional life as remote work, daycare shutdowns, quarantine periods, and more made any sustained separation of those things impossible. It was a lot, but this did help me share more of myself with the promotores than I might have previously. They didn't just get to know me as a white researcher attending their meetings. They got to know me as a mother who attended meetings on the floor of her son's room while playing with him, rocking him to sleep, and periodically turning off her camera to breastfeed him. They got to know me as I contributed to conversations, shared resources, and met with small groups of them for different projects. And I got to know them as they shared about their work, struggles, and communities along the way. They taught me that it was good to bring my full self to our work together as any separation would have further distanced us and negatively impacted how I might learn from them about parenting, reproductive justice, and making research meaningful.

One day while discussing how academics can make higher education more accessible, Maria asked whether I could do a writing class for the promotores someday. I was interested but unsure how it might work in relation to my other teaching responsibilities. And while I did teach writing, I had not ever taught it in Spanish. The idea was general at the time: provide access to something many of them might not have had access to before and do it in a way that fits within their schedule and interests. We spent months talking through options for this class as something that could help the promotores write their own stories. We regularly mentioned the idea to the group of promotores to get a sense of interest and invite feedback. I also drew from what I had learned from the promotores in my research thus far to develop a course design that might resonate with their experiences and interests.

So, during the fall 2021 semester, I facilitated a community writing class in Spanish with a small group of promotores via Zoom. The course design was informed by reproductive justice pedagogy (Ross), community literacy studies (Alvarez; Pritchard), and key concepts about confianza from my research with them. While the class began as a weekly group meeting, we ended up shifting to one-on-one meetings for the second half of the semester since that was what the students preferred. This preference was in part because of their busy schedules but also because of the sensitive things they were working through in their stories. They all had a clear sense of who they wanted to write for and what impact they wanted to have, but many of them had not shared certain parts of their stories with others before then. As we began to enter into confianza with each other, the promotores opened up about deep and difficult topics with their own experiences with relationships, immigration, and reproductive justice. I mostly served as someone to listen, support, and give recommendations for getting their story written down in a way that was guided by their own goals for it. The class began with ten students and ended with six. Those six writers continued working with me on their stories after the class ended to prepare them for a website and public humanities project we were co-creating called Cuentos de Confianza.

The initial idea for Cuentos began the spring before the class began as Maria and I discussed ideas for helping the promotores share their stories with others beyond the class. One of my PhD students, Danielle Koepke, was interning with me at the time to help with conceptualizing some sort of public programming with my research as part of the fellowship I had received. At that point, my research goals and plans for this community writing class began to blend. Danielle and I discussed a variety of ideas for providing an opportunity to publicly share stories, but every step of the way we kept coming back to: what do the promotores want and how can we create something that meets their goals? We went into the fall semester sharing the idea for the website as an option for the writers in the class, but also with the recognition that it might not come to fruition if none of them wanted to contribute to it. And as I said many times, we had to be okay with that. What we learned was that the six promotores who completed the class did want to share stories with members of their families, their communities, and other audiences for them to better understand what it is that they do as promotores and to inspire others. We navigated uncertainty about who the project "belonged" to—My university? PPWI? The writers, themselves?—but ultimately did our best to keep insisting that it be something in the middle–a collaboration of sorts that kept the interests of the writers at the heart of it and that didn't let university or organizational interests take control of decision making and design. Through conversations with the writers in the class, and with the help of an undergraduate student, Juan Arevalo, we developed a bilingual—Spanish-English—website that would host stories written by promotores de salud about their work and experiences with reproductive justice (see https://www.cuentosdeconfianza.com). We launched the site at a community event that focused on our primary audience from the start: the promotores' family, friends, and supporters. We held the event at a high school on the south side of Milwaukee in June 2022, and over 70 people came to eat, connect, and learn about the project.

While this all sounds very neat and successful, the process was anything but. Many weeks were filled with stress and uncertainty for me as I took on my new role of coordinating this community writing project we had dreamed up. I constantly checked in with the writers to be sure I was supporting them in the ways they needed and that we were developing the website in a way that reflected their interests and goals. And even at the website launch when it felt like all our hard work had resulted in a beautiful product, I realized that it was just the beginning of something more. We would need to develop educational materials to help introduce people to the project and encourage certain kinds of engagement with the stories, we would want to get community feedback on how they were receiving the stories, and we would need to add resources as specific issues that came up in the stories—like domestic violence and pregnancy loss—might resonate with readers who could use extra support with those issues. As this project keeps evolving, so does my orientation to the "work" that I'm doing. I don't always know how to delineate what it is that's my community-engaged research versus teaching versus something else these days…but what I do know is that it feels meaningful and driven by good relations.

From Access to Refusal: Remaking University-Community Collaboration

Caroline Gottschalk Druschke

On a recent morning, I joined a very small meeting. Three professors, myself included. Three members of a newly formed watershed council. And two representatives from a small nonprofit, middle-women who had worked to connect the two groups. It had taken the better part of two years to even get to that point. Potential attendees had been screened out to keep things as intimate as possible. Our agenda was focused on testing the waters: feeling each other out to decide whether or not this group of faculty based in Wisconsin's state capital might have something to offer the efforts of this growing watershed council in the rural southwestern portion of the state. The council members introduced themselves and their goals. Our faculty trio introduced ourselves, our methodologies, our community connections. I explained that I had collaborated in the past with watershed councils in Iowa and Rhode Island, had recently returned home to the Midwest, and had found comfort not so much in Madison, but in the creeks and communities I'd connected with across southwest Wisconsin through time spent researching and teaching about accelerating flooding in local waters. The council members listened intently. And then one of my faculty colleagues interjected with a final comment: "Oh wait. We should also mention. We're not trying to publish out of this. We're not thinking about it as research. We just want to see if we can support your work." The mood in the room shifted almost immediately. The members of the watershed council registered surprise and relief.

For good reason.

Since its founding in 1848, in part as a promotional strategy to attract white settlers—like me—to the newly established state of Wisconsin, the University of Wisconsin-Madison—my home institution—has built its ethos around academic intervention in the lives of community members around the state. In a 1905 speech, University President Charles Van Hise introduced what has come to be known and celebrated as "The Wisconsin Idea," describing the university as existing, "for the service of the state," so that, "the knowledge and wisdom of the generations, as well as the achievements of today, may reach all parts of the state." Van Hise concluded his speech with the oft-repeated sentiment, "I shall never be content until the beneficent influence of the University reaches every family of the state." That sentiment sits at the center of our institution, guiding extension initiatives, offered in marketing and recruitment materials, considered in reviews for promotion, named professorships, and fellowships.

Much less repeated is the fact of Van Hise's long-standing advocacy for eugenics, and its deep connection with his advocacy for the Wisconsin Idea. This problematic history is foundational to my focus here: the university's largely unquestioned belief in its intervention in non-university lives and lands as inherent good. Whether grounded in beneficent public service, which it unquestionably takes in many forms, or in leveraging university "experts" for policies like involuntary "sterilization of defectives," encoded in state law from 1913 to 1963, thanks in part to Van Hise's efforts, purportedly to support the "public good" (Vecoli, Dept. of Genetics).

The university was quite literally founded on a demand for access: access to Ho-Chunk lands in the area long known as Teejop that begrudgingly host our campus; access to over 235,000 acres of Menominee and Ojibwe homelands across a huge swath of the northern half of the land now known as Wisconsin converted into university revenue through the Morrill Act of 1862; access to study subjects across the state and now world; access to intellectual property; access to graduate student labor; access to student athletes' bodies. The list goes on.

My point here is not a particular indictment of UW-Madison, at least not more than any other university; UW isn't exceptional in this regard. The entire U.S. land grant university system is founded on and with stolen Native land (la paperson; Lee and Ahtone). From the 272 enslaved individuals sold by the Jesuits in 1838 to fund Georgetown University (Swarns), to Cornell University's speculation in Wisconsin tribal lands that netted the university a $5 million endowment (Gates), to Stanford University's 1971 prison experiment (Reicher et al.), to Arizona State University's 1990 Havasupai DNA study (Shaffer), to Harvard University obtaining private therapy records of a sexual abuse plaintiff and disclosing those records to the defendant, a story that made the news just as I began drafting this essay (Flaherty). Universities depend on access, for their infrastructure and intellect. And my point here is that these examples of abuses related to access and knowledge production aren't a perversion of the academic enterprise; they are a central imperative.

As I began my academic career as a graduate student at the University of Illinois at Chicago [UIC], I was attracted to community-based learning precisely because, in what I consider its best version, it resists this extractive impulse and works, instead, to support community-led initiatives by facilitating access to university resources. Because community-based work often doesn't fit neatly into the consumptive machinery of academia–it's slow and inefficient, often prioritizing process over product, or creating a product that's not well-valued within university structures–I often found myself at UIC and then as a faculty member at the University of Rhode Island as a liaison and advocate for community needs. In the watershed work I mentioned at the outset, for instance, we have invested hours, months, and now years getting to know each other and considering how we might work together for mutual benefit; two years in, this work still emphasizes process not product. In another example, my Rhode Island undergraduates worked with a Providence watershed council and elementary school to revise their riverine education modules and host an environmental education event on a local river. These activities generated local interest, and did important work to connect community members to their neglected rivers, but this isn't work that gets filed under "research" on a faculty CV. These efforts took a large amount of extra labor to convince university administrators and colleagues that this work was valuable and appropriate, something that should be taught, funded, and supported even if it sat outside of academia's consumptive logics. Without ignoring long-standing and important critiques of some forms of service learning as forced, paternalistic, or uncritical (reviewed in Mitchell, 2008), community-driven collaboration, when done well–a "well" that must be determined by community partners (Cruz and Bakken) and must incorporate an explicit critical focus on justice (Gordon da Cruz)—has worked to exist outside the consumptive structures I critiqued above.

But as community engagement is brought more properly into the center of the academic enterprise—e.g. increasing emphases on knowledge co-production and citizen science in scientific RFPs; university interest in public humanities initiatives; field components in courses across disciplines—I want to suggest that this current attention—an interest that borders on fetishization—has huge potential for harm. And I want to argue that university faculty like me committed to community-university collaboration need to use our relative institutional power to continue to allow for access–funneling university resources towards community-driven efforts—but also taking definitive steps to support refusal, which I understand from Eve Tuck and K. Wayne Yang, through Audra Simpson, as "not just as a 'no,' but as a type of investigation into 'what you need to know and what I refuse to write in' (Simpson 72)." This refusal is two-fold: refusal on the part of non-academic communities to "write in" "what you need to know," but also my own refusal as an academic researcher, what Tuck and Yang present as "a refusal to do research, or a refusal within research, as a way of thinking about humanizing researchers" (223).

I have felt a seismic shift in my role in recent years from access to refusal. Much of my time at UW-Madison has been spent working in collaboration with non-university partners on a community-driven oral history project—Stories from the Flood—focused on supporting community healing from increasingly frequent and severe flooding in southwestern Wisconsin with an eye towards moving forward in an increasingly flood-filled future ("Stories from the Flood"). My role in that work has no doubt centered my ability to access resources for the project: securing roughly $50,000 in grant funding for the project from inside and outside the university, communicating with the press and funding agencies, nominating my community partner for monetary awards, designing and teaching community-based learning courses to support the project, accessing university software to create public-facing materials, leveraging departmental and college funds to pay students to support project StoryMaps and findings reports, using university vehicles to transport story gatherers, paying for meals and tour buses, storing project materials on university servers, leading student fellowships and independent studies to support the project. But just as much, that work has been about protecting–and sometimes failing to protect–community storytellers, project organizers, and the project itself from extraction at community members' request: resisting an impulse towards data collection, refusing requests for access to flood-affected community members, and stepping outside of the research-making enterprise ("Cultivating Empathy on the Eve of a Pandemic"). All the while, we are trying to balance access and refusal to co-create a path forward acutely attentive to the potential harms of community research (Tuhiwai Smith; Tuck and Yang).

To come back to the vignette that opened this short essay, I don't know where that watershed conversation will go, and that's part of what matters about it. We've promised to meet again when a colleague and I make the five-hour round trip to attend one of the watershed council's meetings early next month. And we'll take it from there. This is slow, deliberate work that defies university timelines and logics. It's work that focuses on relation, not production. Our trio of faculty are committed to doing that because of our shared orientations and commitments. But we also have the luxury of undertaking this work given the protections of our various positions: we're white settler academics, two of us full professors, one emeritus. It's not that we have less work to do otherwise: two of us run research centers on campus, we teach, we advise, we research, we parent. But we can push on academic expectations with much less risk. And we must.

For me, that means getting myself in front of department chairs, center directors, deans, program officers, and fellow faculty to champion these ideas about access, harm, equity, and refusal. Contributing to a revision of our departmental tenure guidelines that more accurately captures and celebrates engagement work. Supporting, guiding, and learning from the work of junior scholars through manuscript and grant reviews, lecture invitations, tenure and promotion letters, conference panels, and award nominations. Regularly serving on federal grant review panels so that I can express what I know will be an unpopular opinion. Offering to run defense for community partners who are burned out on university contact. Writing job descriptions that reflect these orientations. Working to stay up to date on always unfolding best practices in ethical community engagement. And pushing myself into discomfort (Gottschalk Druschke): initiating uncomfortable boundary setting conversations with partners, students, and colleagues; tolerating continued—and warranted—hazing about my connection to the university; making regular five-hour round trips for in-person meetings after long days of work; existing through chronic outsider-ness; advocating for this work with higher ups; and so on. Moments like these offer powerful opportunities for remaking university-community collaboration in ways that support good relations–relations that support community-driven efforts, relations that refuse the expectations of the university, relations that nourish those involved–and make space inside of and despite exploitative university structures for collaboration and refusal.

Remembering Forward

To conclude, we forgo the typical synthesis and reiteration of what all we said in each of our pieces in order to bring this work back to you–members of our CLJ community. We, academics in community with each other based on shared interests in community and literacy, must talk about issues of access and justice among ourselves. Having these conversations here, with each other, decreases the burdens we place on community partners by asking them to tell us how they want to be accessed, or not, or assuming that all's well if we haven't heard otherwise.

By way of example: while we were revising this very article, one of us—Cagle—was asked by a colleague at her institution to consult on a project working with victims of a very recent flood. Because of Caroline's work with community members who had experienced catastrophic flooding, Cagle was able to talk through with her how to best support this colleague, which may end up meaning advising the colleague not to proceed with the project. We talked about some potential complications. Have flood-affected community members invited this colleague in to support their recovery? Are the flood and the trauma it continues to create too fresh for academics to start asking communities questions about it? Does the colleague have training in mental health and trauma response, and do they plan to collaborate with someone who does? Are there measures in place to make sure this colleague remains connected to flood-affected communities long-term, even after their students move on to new classes and interests? This moment is precisely why we need this conversation within our CLJ community, and why we offer you our four distinct stories within a single article. It is not despite, but because the four of us–and any number of readers–occupy different personal and institutional positions, that we can offer each other support as we navigate specific projects and requests for access.

We close by encouraging you, our colleagues, to remember forward, that is, to consider what encountering these learning experiences has brought up for you and to apply it to future contexts purposefully. After all, we are in the midst of doing that same work. To assist you with remembering forward, we return to the open-ended questions that prompted our reflections about access. We hope these questions can help guide you in thinking deeply about how you community, how you want to community, how you protect your communities, and how that affects your professional practice.

- How can we, both we specifically and academics in general, make use of the Cultural Rhetorics pillars of story, relationality, constellation, and decolonization to foster good relations in our shared work?
- How can we co-create new stories about what it means to do this work in community?
- What risks associated with research and co-production of knowledge might marginalized members incur via providing access for outsiders to their communities?
- What harm might we—and *do* we—cause in our community-based work?

- How might community building with languages other than English help us deepen our understanding of good relations?
- How can we work against the impulse–and often the expectation–to "research"?

Works Cited

"Access." *Dictionary.com*, n.d., https://www.dictionary.com/browse/access.

Absolon (Minogiizhigokwe), Kathleen E. *Kaandossiwin, 2nd ed.: How We Come to Know: Indigenous Re-Search Methodologies*. Fernwood Publishing, 2021.

Alaska Native Knowledge Network. "Alaska Natives Earned Doctorate." *Google Docs*, 19 March 2022, https://docs.google.com/document/d/1JJQIuhPq3U9owbSL8O2-haYhbryE8aZWWRUslrNbBB8/edit?fbclid=IwAR2iddwDJX-fu4ZQZC2-eDsCnF1DciBbTH2MdUUr8XB-F0bNOn5iIKBCxd3s.

Alvarez, Steven. *Community Literacies En Confianza: Learning from Bilingual After-School Programs*. National Council of Teachers of English, 2017.

Bloom-Pojar, Rachel, and Maria Barker. "The role of confianza in community-engaged work for reproductive justice." *Reflections* 20.2 (2020): 84-101.

Cruz, Evelyn, and Lori Bakken. "Community Guidelines for Engaging with Researchers and Evaluators: A Toolkit for Community Agencies, Organizations and Coalitions." May 2020, https://ictr.wisc.edu/documents/community-guidelines-for-engaging-with-researchers-and-evaluators/.

Department of Genetics. University of Wisconsin, n.d. "Historical Issues: Grappling with Our Past." https://genetics.wisc.edu/historical-issues-grappling-with-our-past/. Accessed 25 Sept. 2022.

Edenfield, Avery C., Ryan Cheek, and Sam Clem. "Trans* Vulnerability and Digital Research Ethics: A Qubit Ethical Analysis of Transparency Activism." *The 39th ACM International Conference on Design of Communication*. 2021.

Flaherty, Colleen. "Without Her Consent." *Inside Higher Education*, 10 Feb. 2022, https://www.insidehighered.com/news/2022/02/10/harvard-allegedly-obtained-students-outside-therapy-records.

Gates, Paul W. *Wisconsin Pine Lands of Cornell University*. State Historical Society of Wisconsin, 1943.

Gordon da Cruz, Cynthia. "Critical community-engaged scholarship: Communities and universities striving for racial justice." *Peabody Journal of Education* 92.3 (2017): 363-384.

Gottschalk Druschke, Caroline, et al. "Stories from the Flood: Promoting Healing and Fostering Policy Change Through Storytelling, Community Literacy, and Community-based Learning." *Community Literacy Journal* 16.2 (2022): 35.

Gottschalk Druschke, Caroline, et al. "Cultivating Empathy on the Eve of a Pandemic." *Reflections: A Journal of Community-Engaged Writing and Rhetoric*. 21.1. (2022).

Gottschalk Druschke, Caroline. "Agonistic Methodology: A Rhetorical Case Study in Agricultural Stewardship." In Rai, Candice, and Caroline Gottschalk Druschke, editors. *Field Rhetoric : Ethnography, Ecology, and Engagement in the Places of Persuasion*. University of Alabama Press, 2018.

Hamraie, Aimi. *Building access: Universal design and the politics of disability*. University of Minnesota Press, 2017.

Itchuaqiyaq, Cana Uluak, and Breeanne Matheson. "Decolonial dinners: Ethical Considerations of "Decolonial" Metaphors in TPC." *Technical Communication Quarterly* 30.3 (2021): 298-310.

Kimmerer, Robin W. *Braiding Sweetgrass: Indigenous Wisdom, Scientific Knowledge and the Teachings of Plants* (First Paperback edition). Milkweed Editions, 2015.

la paperson. *A Third University Is Possible*. University of Minnesota Press, 2017.

Lee, Robert, and Tristan Ahtone. "Land-Grab Universities." *High Country News*, March 2020. https://www.hcn.org/issues/52.4/indigenous-affairs-education-land-grab-universities

Powell, Malea, et al. "Our story begins here: Constellating cultural rhetorics." *Enculturation: A Journal of Rhetoric, Writing, and Culture* 25 (2014): 1-28.

Pritchard, Eric D. *Fashioning Lives: Black Queers and the Politics of Literacy*. Southern Illinois University Press, 2017.

Rai, Candice, and Caroline Gottschalk Druschke, editors. *Field Rhetoric : Ethnography, Ecology, and Engagement in the Places of Persuasion*. University of Alabama Press, 2018.

Reicher, Stephen, S. Alexander Haslam, and Jay J. Van Bavel. "Time to change the story." *The Psychologist* 31.8 (2018): 2-3.

Ross, Loretta J. "Teaching Reproductive Justice: An Activist's Approach." In Perlow, Olivia N, et al., editors. *Black Women's Liberatory Pedagogies: Resistance, Transformation, and Healing Within and Beyond the Academy*. Palgrave Macmillian, 2018, 159-180.

Rudolf, Margaret. "Understanding How to Improve Climate Change Co-Production of Knowledge Projects with Alaska Native Communities." *ACCAP*, n.d., https://uaf-accap.org/research-activities/understanding-coproduction-ak-native-communities/

Shaffer, Mark. "Havasupai Blood Samples Misused." *Indian Country Today*, 12 Sept. 2018, https://indiancountrytoday.com/archive/havasupai-blood-samples-misused.

Simpson, Audra. "On Ethnographic Refusal: Indigeneity, 'Voice,' and Colonial Citizenship." *Junctures* 9 (2007): 67–80.

SisterSong. "Reproductive Justice." *Sistersong.net*, n.d., https://www.sistersong.net/reproductive-justice.

Smith, Linda Tuhiwai. *Decolonizing Methodologies : Research and Indigenous Peoples*. Third edition., Third ed., Zed Books, 2021.

Sparrow, Elena, et al. "Developing and Implementing a Culture of Diversity, Equity, and Inclusion at an International Research Center in an Arctic University to Build Trusting, Caring and Professional Relationships Across International Research Communities." *AGU Fall Meeting Abstracts*. Vol. 2021. 2021.

Swarns, Rachel L. "272 slaves were sold to save Georgetown. What does it owe their descendants?" *The New York Times*, 16 April 2016, https://www.nytimes.com/2016/04/17/us/georgetown-university-search-for-slave-descendants.html.

Todd, Zoe S. "Fish Philosophy." *Critical Indigenous Fish Philosophy*, n.d., https://zoesctodd.wordpress.com/.

Tuck, Eve, and K. Wayne Yang. "R-words: Refusing Research." In Paris, Django, and Maisha T Winn, editors. *Humanizing Research: Decolonizing Qualitative Inquiry with Youth and Communities*. SAGE, 2014.

Van Hise, Charles. "Address before Press Association." www.wisc.edu, Feb. 1905, https://www.wisc.edu/pdfs/VanHiseBeneficentAddress.pdf.

Vecoli, Rudolph J. "Sterilization: A Progressive Measure?" *Wisconsin Magazine of History* 43 (1960): 190–202.

Author Bios

Cana Uluak Itchuaqiyaq is a tribal member of the Noorvik Native Community in NW Alaska and is an assistant professor of professional and technical writing at Virginia Tech. Her research addresses how mainstream modes of academic practice often perpetuates the marginalization of underrepresented scholars and communities and consequentially interferes with equity. Her research combines her academic background in both the digital humanities and physical sciences and currently centers on creating accessible online databases of Inuit knowledges and developing natural language processing techniques to extract climate change data from Inuit narratives. She is an author on the upcoming *National Climate Assessment 5*, Alaska Chapter, and serves on several boards, including the Caleb Scholars Program, Arctic Research Consortium of the United States, *Kairos: A Journal of Rhetoric, Technology, and Pedagogy*, and *Communication Design Quarterly*.

Caroline Gottschalk Druschke (@creekthinker) is a professor of rhetoric in the department of English at the University of Wisconsin-Madison, where she also serves as Chair of Water@UW, an umbrella organization that connects water scholars across the UW-Madison campus and across the state. Gottschalk Druschke's research, teaching, and community work are centrally rooted in relations to people and place across southwestern Wisconsin and organized around the questions of how people change rivers and how rivers change people. Gottschalk Druschke has presented internationally on her work, published widely across rhetorical studies and freshwater science and management, and received fellowships from the Andrew W. Mellon Foundation, the US Environmental Protection Agency, and AAUW and funding from the National Science Foundation and the National Park Service.

Lauren Cagle is an Associate Professor of Writing, Rhetoric, and Digital Studies and Affiliate Faculty in Environmental and Sustainability Studies and Appalachian Studies at the University of Kentucky. She teaches courses in scientific, environmental, and technical communication, and her research focuses on overlaps among digital rhetorics, research ethics, and scientific, environmental, and technical communication.

Cagle frequently works with local and regional environmental and technical practitioners; her current collaborative partners include the Kentucky Division for Air Quality, the Kentucky Geological Survey, the University of Kentucky Recycling Program, and The Arboretum, State Botanical Garden of Kentucky. Cagle's work has appeared in *Technical Communication Quarterly*, the *Journal of Technical Writing and Communication*, *Rhetoric Review*, and *Computers & Composition*.

Rachel Bloom-Pojar is an Associate Professor with the program in Public Rhetorics and Community Engagement at the University of Wisconsin-Milwaukee. Her research examines communication about health with a specific focus on the rhetorical practices of Latinx communities, interpreters, and *promotores de salud* (health promoters). She was a 2020-2021 Mellon/ACLS Scholars and Society Fellow with Planned Parenthood of Wisconsin, Inc. (PPWI) and has continued working with the PPWI *promotores de salud* in various capacities related to education and research. Her published work has appeared in the NCTE Studies in Writing and Rhetoric Series, *Reflections*, *Present Tense*, the *Journal of Applied Communication Research*, and *Methodologies for the Rhetoric of Health and Medicine* (Routledge).

Book and New Media Reviews

From the Book and New Media Review Editor's Desk

Jessica Shumake, Editor
University of Notre Dame

For those making winter reading lists, the reviews featured here offer some thoughtful suggestions. I am grateful to Geoffrey Clegg, Kristen A. Ruccio, and Jagadish Paudel for their perceptive reviews. Albert Maysles, a filmmaker, in an interview with film studies scholar Frank Verano, said that his philosophy as a cinematographer is to "love thy neighbor" (158). I share Maysles' philosophy both as a section editor for *CLJ* and as a writing teacher. Love for one's neighbor requires respect and understanding, but it mostly requires an effort to "get it right" (Maysles 158). The writers whose reviews are featured in this issue, got it right in terms of their attention to detail and effort to capture and transmit their reading experiences. I hope their voices come through loud and clear and their reviews grab attention and spur curiosity.

Works Cited

Verano, Frank. "'Direct cinema is anything but a fly on the wall': a conversation with Albert Maysles." *Doc on-line*, no. 20, 2016, pp. 153–161.

Rhetoric Inc: Ford's Filmmaking and the Rise of Corporatism

Timothy Johnson
The Pennsylvania State University Press, 2020, 227 pp.

Reviewed by Geoffrey Clegg
Midwestern State University

In *Rhetoric Inc.: Ford's Filmmaking and the Rise of Corporatism*, Timothy Johnson presents the narrative of how corporate powers have structured themselves as indispensable from economic, civic, and discursive life. Scholars of communication studies, rhetoric, writing studies, and film will find that Johnson's use of incorporational rhetoric makes a firm argument for why we have a toxic relationship with how we talk about the intersections of business, enterprise, and rhetoric. To structure his larger arguments, Johnson pays specific attention to the Ford Motor Company's use of instructional films, mostly produced in-house by the Ford Film Company until World War II, to shape the discursive space of American economic and political life. Through a careful viewing of the film archives, Johnson presents an engaging study into how corporations have firmly cemented their place in America's overarching capitalist system and our national identity.

Readers of the *Community Literacy Journal* may not find the title and topic inviting; however, Johnson's book will present them with useful strategies for reading film and thinking about concepts related to power projection, identity formation, and even the role of omission in shaping discourse. Ford's films from the silent era all the way to the mid-1950s are an effective means of viewing literacies because film is a space of both examining how past generations absorbed the dominant discourses of labor, immigration, and working-class education. Like written discursive materials, film allows for the crafting of narrative, decisive choices made through editing and exclusion, and exhibiting specific themes that shape rhetoric. Johnson's work effectively takes us into an emergent space of the early 20th century to explore a literacy form as it slowly conceptualizes itself from the silent era until the post-war economic boom.

The book's introduction argues that the 2008 automotive bailout was not just a push to save jobs and economic prosperity; instead, automotive manufactures carefully crafted a larger economic, political, and rhetorical project meant to cement themselves as integral to American society. Specifically, Johnson highlights how "economies are powerful rhetorical constructs built to a large degree by larger corporate institutions and produced as controlling narratives 'incorporated' to their core" (5). These economies, both monetarily and rhetorically based, provide a larger launching point to understanding how our techcentric knowledge economy came to dominate the post-industrial makeup of many first-world countries. By digging through Ford, Johnson seeks to answer how we have let companies like Alphabet, Amazon (and the real moneymaker Amazon Web Services), and Apple create narratives central to their monolithic needs and change those narratives when confronted by problems within society. It is from this position that Johnson turns to the idea of incorporational rhetoric that he defines as "an approach to analyzing the large, distributed configurations of materials, texts, and ideas brought together by immense corporations like Ford" (6). Incoporational rhetorics go beyond the educational films meant to be distributed to willing theaters since companies can now ply their trade via social media, websites, and within the traditional print media and movies. Johnson sees these spaces as "unique enough to warrant a bracketed, named iteration of rhetorical practice," which is meant to accent Antonio Gramsci's theory of hegemony (6). The ways in which companies lay the groundwork for their legitimacy—not to mention their power to persuade government officials—is primary to incorporational rhetoric as it reifies their ability to position themselves as a public good rather than a strictly capitalist scheme.

Johnson's first chapter foregrounds the melding of Progressive Era educational expansion—as captured through various reforms from Thomas Dewey to the integration of onsite workplace schooling—with the increased industrialization of American life. To frame this, Johnson uses a July 1916 Ford event that combined the pageantry of schooling with the then ever-present call for assimilation where American flags, foreign workers who arrived to work on the assembly line, and a banner promoting the Ford Motor Company English School presented a facade for democracy (28–29). Worker education, especially that of those not born into American culture and language, was pure indoctrination, which, as Johnson points out, focused on citizenship and language acquisition with those who took to the program given both citizenship and a chance to advance into the burgeoning pre-war middle class. In a way, the student *cum* workers of the Ford plant were in themselves a commodified engine of the economy set to be built on a working line and sold to both the public and future employees in videos.

The turn to Ford's silent film-era educational movies offers one of the more brilliant parts of the chapter as Johnson dissects the popularity of the *Ford Educational Weekly*—later becoming the *Ford Educational Library*—in both theaters and among the press. What is striking is the way in which the films were labeled as educational and distributed to schools under the auspices of both industrial and civic use in the classroom. These films pre-date the later post WWII Coronet films, which also focused on similar themes of good citizenship and were marketed as educational training, and featured the same "homogenized national experience of visual learning as theatregoers, workers, and students received identical lessons" (34). What Ford crafts is a modified version of reality meant to stimulate the imaginations of the viewers but at the same time indoctrinate their worldviews to match each subsequent film. In a way, the early Ford films were less about strict education and more propaganda for the audiences to ingest in order to alter the makeup of social, political, and labor life. Johnson sees these films through mise-en-scéne, which he reads through Jacques Rivette's conception of the term to mean a rhetorical tool used to observe the complex assemblages of people, place, and networks. Rivette's framework helps further Johnson's incorporational rhetorical argument through the complexity that these films present on an educational level. On one hand, instructional films were meant for emulation of form, training, and potential. Yet, Johnson argues that Ford's films were sites of the modernized shift away from localized labor towards a transformed, mechanized, and unified industrial similitude. What we might get from Johnson's masterful reading of these films is the paired modernization of education—worker and school education—that still prevails: a sterile, one-size-fits-all form of indoctrination that throws out ingenuity and local knowledge in favor of standardization and corporate oversight.

Chapter two highlights how Ford uses the hagiographical metamontage, *As Dreams Come True* (1921) to present the ur-narrative of both Ford the person and Ford the company. The goal of *As Dreams Come True*, in Johnson's view, is to "presen[t] the aspirations of its figurehead to naturalize a larger and often turbulent, boom-and-bust structure for economic cycles" in order to "obfuscate elements of labor on the assembly line" as well as "recast an influx of money into new forms of capital including military prowess, mass consumption, and leisure" (65). To unravel this film, Johnson draws upon a diverse framework of theoretical perspectives ranging from Casey Boyle, Gayatari Spivak, and Gilles Deleuze in order to deliver the sharp message that "[p]erfecting a new reality was, as *As Dreams Come True* makes clear, at the heart of the Fordist project" (69). *As Dreams Come True* serves as a kind of economic *topoi* that captures the world Ford wants his audience—plant workers and theatergoers alike—to internalize through their imagined selves. To achieve this, the film captures two economic realities (the meritocratic rise of Ford and the regime of labor at Ford's plants) and twists them into a propagandic assemblage meant to exhibit aspirational qualities to be emulated by the audience.

Chapter three takes us from the imagined foundations of emergent American economic life to constructing the spatial dimensions of Ford's automotive industry. The focus in this chapter moves from *As Dreams Come True* to the follow-up films like *Good Roads* (1921) and *Village-Industries* (1932), to which Johnson uses the expansive highway system as a metaphor for the circulation of capital, bodies, labor, and commercial products. The use of scenic backgrounds as opposed to city spaces presents an imagined assemblage of the real as structured through freedom. It is here that Ford's films bifurcate into scenes from Michigan villages to vast American National Parks. The use of villages like Milford and Hayden Mills, Michigan are meant to provide the larger networks of industry that act as "intermediary space[s] between the urban and rural" (106). Whereas prior spaces would have been independent from incorporation, these films present them as proximal nodes in the gears of industry and ultimately tied to the larger facets of the growing transportation network. Later films like *Fairy Fantasy in Stone: Bryce National Park* (1937) expand upon the nationwide increase in visits to the National Park system. Ford's travelogues connect viewers to the larger America they are beginning to visit, if not imagine, as part of the network of interconnected highway systems. Johnson concludes that the intermixing of National Park vistas and vehicles triggers both physical and emotional reactions that dictate an imagined life with access to both possible. Specifically, now travel is a consumable product.

Chapter four pivots from imagined landscapes to Ford's attempt to build relationships with consumer audiences through the spectacle of the 1934 World's Fair films. In contrast to the Depression Era films produced by The Film and Photo League that fought for the regulating of labor practices, Ford's film presents a serene counter to the economic anxieties of the public deep into the Depression years. Johnson's shot for shot readings of *Ford and a Century of Progress* (1934) and *Rhapsody in Steel* (1934) pairs each film with the notions of the sublime. Each film is categorized differently—*Ford and a Century of Progress* stands as a montage of images meant to invoke escapism while *Rhapsody in Steel* presents an absurd bread and circuses effect—but their main focus is on presenting a narrative counter to the feelings of the general public of the time. Unlike previous films meant to showcase training, the World's Fair films are an exercise in an "overwhelming overlap of multiple sensory experiences coordinated through their own spectacular features," which are intended to subdue the audience (147). Johnson uses these two films to foreshadow the last film of the chapter, *Harvest of the Years* (1940), where the abstract, sensory images are replaced by a cohesive film where montages are meant to show both the beginning of economic and emotional recoveries of the spectator.

Ford's wartime film strategy shifts from spectacle vis-a-vis the viewer's experiential enchantment to a more strident argument for a managed technocratic society. Chapter five spends significant time examining the shift to wartime production with the outwardly propagandist piece *Women on the Warpath* (1943). The film is an extension of both the war effort and corporate management. Johnson frames this through the tripartite forms of managerial, masculine, and colonial gazes that objectify bodies in motion as they work in tandem with machines (157). One of the more compelling arguments made in the chapter concerns the late-stage editing and omission of international and gendered labor in favor of the "white, male, Western executive" as savior narrative shown in Ford films during the war years (180). While the section on editing is relatively short, Johnson points us to the belief that the "final editing in film can offer important insights into the ideological positions being taken by a filmmaker—these editing decisions inform us of what a rhetor-editor finds worthy of seeing" (181). The choices editors make, as part of their process, help to shape wartime attitudes towards Ford's manufacturing in other countries: Germany gets a small focus before American entrance into the war, Sweden and Finland are sites where the male and female body are meant to be observed and sexualized, and Egypt is space where the American, neé Fordist, way of life has proven successful. Each of these choices are part of the larger editorial scope of the film and their selections speak volumes about their utility to the ultimate mission of corporate culture through their observation of Ford's success.

In his conclusion, Johnson suggests that the automotive corporations had ultimately proven a simple point in the leadup to the 2008 bailout: they were too big to fail because they were integral to American society. Effectively, companies like Ford circulated an incorporational rhetoric, which crafted a networked understanding of their own value throughout the 20th century that "work[ed] to subvert or reshape what we traditionally consider rhetorical action" (185). *Rhetoric Inc.* reminds us that the appeals made by corporations and corporate interests are grounded in a long-term political project undertaken to persuade the public through visual rather than written rhetoric. If we are to better understand why corporations have a stranglehold on discourse in this country, we must look at how each corporation has used incorporational rhetorics to define their value and need in daily life beyond just the consumption of their goods. As Johnson articulates through the book, Ford's corporate style of rhetoric is one that is carried out over a long period of time and uses a multitude of genres to define its mission.

Johnson's book reminds us that so much of the corporatist rhetoric we see today is based on a series of obfuscations meant to divert our attention away from labor conditions, stagnant wages as well as loss of pensions, and gendered inequity in favor of corporately crafted imagined ideals of community, life, and structure. For literacy scholars, chapter one offers perhaps the best source material for potential use because Johnson spends significant time on the ways in which film was used as an instructional tool for a variety of audiences. Film and communication scholars will get the most out of the subsequent chapters (chapters two and three, especially) where Johnson focuses specifically on the intersections of theory and film. Rhetoric scholars will find the whole book worthy for more than just the idea of incorporational rhetoric, as Johnson's major arguments are expertly grounded in a variety of rhetorical theories that present new pathways for future research. Overall, *Rhetoric Inc.* presents scholars many different entry points into how corporations use film, rhetoric, and narrative to create new structures of persuasion that come to dictate modern economic realities.

Women's Ways of Making

Edited by Maureen Daly Goggin and Shirley K Rose
UP of Colorado, 2021, 278 pp.

Reviewed by Kristen A. Ruccio
Arkansas State University

Betsy Greer's statement that "every act of making is an act of revolution," which serves as the epigraph for *Women's Ways of Making*, sets the stage for this edited collection (3). In popular culture, making often becomes attached to the maker movement, craft communities, or even DIY culture—and all share a basis in materiality and in creation or reclamation. Yet, many of these makings are specifically stratified by gender, with maker communities skewing to actually reinforce(s) an ingrained culture of "white masculinity in the design and deployment of technology while rhetorically claiming universality" (Britton). Craft communities, particularly yarn craft communities, are often associated with femininity, a view reinforced by the popular *Stitch 'n Bitch* and *The Happy Hooker* series of books by Debbie Stoller. Maureen Daly Goggin and Shirley K Rose, names familiar to readers of the *Community Literacy Journal*, present a wide-ranging collection about making that not only focuses on women's ways of making, but also revolutionizes and makes transparent the labor of knowledge-making by women. The continuous thread running through this collection is "that the three ways of knowing [episteme, techne, and phronesis] emerge from experience and work in harmony as embodied acts" (4).

The collection originated in presentations from the October 2015 Tenth Biennial Feminisms and Rhetorics Conference and represents "selected and revised presentations from that event" (4). While both the conference and the emergent collection hold a variety of makings, they are grounded in the study of "feminist rhetoric and writing studies" (4). As a work grounded in feminisms, the collection focuses on the embodied and practical ways making knowledge occurs. The editors skillfully connect these traditions to a long history of considering "epistemic acts" that represent women's ways of making (4–7). The authors of the thirteen chapters included in the collection represent "scholars at every stage of making their scholarly lives in the academy, from graduate students through established senior faculty members, as well as those outside academia. . .That diversity is purposeful and celebrated here" (6).

And while I have correctly described the collection as "wide-ranging," the organization of the chapters into three sections provides a map for the reader to easily follow through these embodied acts of making.

Rachael A. Ryerson's opening chapter, "Remaking the Female Reproductive Body in *Saga*," gives a brief overview of the typical ways "that women's bodies in comics are typically portrayed in hypersexualized, fetishized ways" (17). Her argument that *Saga*'s representation of female reproductive bodies in abject ways "visually centers and celebrates them, and in the process, ultimately reworks discursive norms for these bodies" (18). Ryerson reminds us that the very presence of pregnant bodies in a comic is remarkable because a pregnant body embodies "that which has been defined as abject" (20). In addition to realistic portrayals of birth, which include excrement and other bodily fluids, Ryerson's argument centers on the fact that *Saga* also includes normalized, nonsexual images of both breastfeeding and miscarriage (31–35). While "norms are in flux," Ryerson concludes, comics such as *Saga* are working to change the possibilities of how female bodies can be represented (37).

The research methods used by the authors in *Women's Ways of Making* are as varied as the topics of that research, and in chapter two, Christine Martorana presents "The Woman Rhetor and Her Body: A Case-Study Analysis of How a Feminist Zinester Constructs Ethos as a Corporeal Experiential Authority." Martorana does a great job of defining terms such as "ethos" and "corporeal experiential authority" for her audience before moving to the analysis. Authorial moves such as this make this text, while deeply scholarly, accessible to a variety of audiences. Martorana argues that *Here. In My Head* "is a feminist perzine: a zine with an explicit dual focus that is both personal and feminist," which makes it a perfect fit for analysis of both aspects of the case study (44). Martorana presents a clear picture of how Cath, the author of the perzine *Here. In My Head*, moves between the personal and the feminist. "The result is a new way of understanding women's ethos and the strategies available to feminist rhetors" (55). Much of Martorana's argument centers on how feminist rhetors need not rely on physical attributes to create ethos, which contrasts interestingly with Holly Fulton-Babicke's piece in chapter three, "Ripped Goddess: New Ways of Making Women's Fitness," who argues that "identities are increasingly enacted in hybrid public/private spaces, such as internet forums" (57). Ripped Goddess is one of these hybrid spaces, which Fulton-Babicke describes as "a vibrant women's fitness group" that "consistently focuses on self-esteem building and exercise as self-care" as much as it focuses on weightlifting (57). This community, she argues, works as a public sphere in which all spectrums of gender are represented, including traditional, transgressive, and cyberfeminist representations of gender (60–62). Fulton-Babicke deftly provides evidence that Ripped Goddess also overturns norms of how an online women's fitness operates, because it is a community focused on building, rather than confining what female identity can be—and indeed what femininity can look like, whether that replicates or transgresses ideas of normative depictions of femininity.

Lorin Shellenberger's contribution "Building Embodied Êthe: Brandi Chastain's Goal Celebration and the Problem of Situated Ethos" uses the example of elite athletes, such as Chastain, to argue that the creation of ethos is not solely dependent on the choices of an individual. Instead, "ethos is determined through a variety of factors, including previous cultural narratives, ongoing media discourses, choices about self-representation, and one's physical body (among others)" (74). She argues that we, as scholars of rhetoric, must attend to these factors, because they "might influence the ability to develop an ethos" (74). Shellenberger offers the term "ēthe" (plural of ethos), to reflect the multiplicity of factors that impact the development of ethos (76). The author uses the image of Chastain's celebration of making a goal to build the argument that Chastain could not build her own ethos in that moment because the image was freighted with cultural expectations, the newness of an image of female joy in that situation, not to mention the still-ongoing discussion of the appropriateness of a female athlete ripping off her shirt—even though that is a common image among male athletes. In the end, the case of Chastain embodies how factors determining ēthe can be imposed *on* the individual rather than chosen by the individual (92, emphasis in original).

Chapters five and six conclude the first section and take yoga as a focus for embodied knowledge making. In "Posed to Emote: Making the Emotional-Embodied Work of Rhetorical Training Observable through Yoga Practice," Jacquelyn E. Hoermann-Elliott recounts her experience of facilitating a Yoga-Zen writing class (96). She focuses on the narratives of three of the students in the class "in order to demonstrate the surprising, often-overlooked role emotions play in embodied writing practices" (96). Hoermann-Elliott provides a literature review about embodied writing and scholarship about the role of yoga in the writing classroom and workshop in this piece—anyone who chooses this subject to research would benefit from reading this piece for the literature review alone. However, the piece also has a deeply personal aspect when the author discusses three of her participants' reactions and writings in the class. Hoermann-Elliott also helpfully provides, in a series of appendices, the course design and learning outcomes, so that readers can design their own course from this piece, which presents the first overtly pedagogical material in the collection. In a shift from the pedagogical to the administrative, Kathleen J. Ryan and Christy I. Wenger take "Yoga as Feminist Techne: Making Space for Administrative Well-Being" as their subject in chapter six. They seek to make their intention clear to "reimagine women's work as writing program administrators (WPAs)" in their contribution (115). Their central claim is that yoga has "profoundly shape[d] how and why we do what we do" and they argue that yoga is "a feminist *techne*, one that provides us a method of doing and making in feminist administration (115, emphasis in original). While there is no shortage of scholarly linkages made in this piece, the writing takes the reader along a narrative path of how each author discovered the impact yoga had on their administrative labor. As a WPA myself, I found their final section "Yoga as a Means of Feminist Intervention" especially relevant. They write: "Yoga consequently helps us approach resilience as a skill that can be learned and applied to WPAing" (125). Anyone who has worked in an administrative position knows that resilience is a skill we all need to maintain well-being.

The beginning of section two provides a completely different research topic in "Elizabeth I and the Rhetoric of the Marriage Crisis," written by Jane Donawerth.

Donawerth argues that "who would marry the queen" was a dominant topic of public discourse during the reign of Elizabeth I (135). The main argument of the piece is that Elizabeth I, instead of being a "master rhetor" who persuaded her audiences by her clever use of rhetoric, was actually a collaborative, interactive, and imitative rhetor who worked with her audience (135–136; 144). Donawerth takes nothing away from the rhetorical skill of Elizabeth I, but does humanize the queen by providing research that points to Elizabeth I's dissatisfaction with her marriage being part of public discourse for twenty-five years.

Chapter eight provides one of the topical swings (while still connecting to the theme of the section) that makes reading this collection compelling; the reader does not have a chance to get bored. Andrea J. Severson writes in "Fleur de Force: Beauty, Creativity, and *YouTube*," of the beauty community on *YouTube* and focuses her research Fleur de Force, a British YouTuber who has "built a highly successful career from her beauty-and-lifestyle-themed-channel, with over 1.4 million subscribers" (150). Severson draws connection among feminist rhetorical practices and creativity in online beauty communities and recounts the history of feminist interventions into these topics (152–156). With the in-depth analysis of Fleur de Force's rhetorical and creative choices, Severson reminds us that online beauty influencers are not just "amateurs sitting around talking about makeup," but are entrepreneurs who make complex business decisions for their own "personal brand" (157). The end of the article predicts, accurately, where future research of beauty vloggers and influencers could lead—the challenges of sponsored content and the interactive element of online influencers and their followers (160). Those debates currently surround the topic of social media-based beauty communities, which shows Severson's considerable foresight.

Kathleen Blake Yancey's chapter, "A Study of Making-Ness: Texts, Memory, and Art," provides a breath of narrative fresh air because it begins with an italicized first-person account that details a break-in at her home and some of the objects that were lost in the process (161). The piece then transitions to non-italicized text and an erudite discussion of scholarship about memorializing loss and the functions of eulogy (162). As a way to memorialize the loss, Yancey created an "artist's book" as a visual account/eulogy—spurred by the CFP for the 2015 Feminisms and Rhetorics Conference, which included a category for exhibition pieces (166–167). Yancey describes the process of creating the exhibition book as "intimidating in a way giving a paper, for me, is not" because of the emotional content and the sharing of a personal event with strangers (167). Yancey shares the process of making the artist's book in personal vignettes that are interspersed with discussions of epistemic creation, Cartesian duality in the Western tradition, and writing from artists about the process of making art. Yancey includes, in a clear and engaging chapter, a vast amount of diverse scholarship. This piece could also serve as a model or inspiration for ways of integrating personal sharing and embodied storytelling into a piece for an academic audience.

The most visually-engaging chapter of the collection is "Red Tent: Creating Art and Our Lives in Jail through Feminist Rhetorics" The piece chronicles The Red Tent Women's Initiative, which "provides a weekly support group for nonviolent female offenders within the Pinellas County Jail in Clearwater, Florida" and is co-authored by

Jill McCracken, Amanda Ellis, Melissa Greene, and Charlese Trower (176). The piece analyzes the incarceration system and how it impacts women in our society, but also discusses empowering and supporting women through groups like Red Tent. The authors' claim that "Red Tent is a mechanism through which feminist rhetoric occurs" is supported through the images, descriptions, and narratives of participants in Red Tent (179). The ways in which the personal narratives about making begin with the creation of objects sewn, yet end with commentary about the incarceration system itself is particularly persuasive. The descriptions of the rhetorical messages of the jail itself—a space designed to decrease intimacy and to punish—in contrast with the Red Tent Room—a space designed to uplift and to create community—exemplify the contrasts between these two spaces (186–190). Scholarship, such as this piece, invites readers from outside academia because it is based in community engagement and in empowerment, which feel relevant to all.

The third and final section opens with another chapter that focuses on the work of WPAs; "Renewing Feminist Perspectives on Women WPAs' Service and Leadership" by Hui Wu and Emily Standridge. The section begins by exploring the central role rhetoric and composition play in the survival of English departments, but end with the transformative potential of WPAs who will likely be shifting the focus and the future of the academy. Their meticulously crafted argument lacks the often-pedantic tone of debates about the professional status of composition, which makes for a refreshing change. For those of us who teach composition and/or who are WPAs, Wu and Standridge's discussion of the ways in which the field has tried to shun the service nature of composition reminds us that our work is largely service-based, but that we should not internalize that as a detriment to our knowledge-making as teachers and as administrators. They conclude by arguing that since leadership work is (and always has been) service work and because WPAs are engaged in leadership every day, there is a unique opportunity and responsibility for WPAs in ". . . transforming the structure of academia. Only after the structure is changed can the academic culture, style of thinking, and labor division change" (216). A weighty charge, indeed, but one that seems possible as this chapter clearly maps that this is making that WPAs have already been doing.

The penultimate chapter, "Other Ways of Making It: Transcending Traditional Academic Trajectories," written by Theresa M. Evans, Linda Hanson, Karen S. Neubauer, and Daneryl Weber requires a disclaimer from me. I hit the academic job market and got my doctorate when I was in my late 40s; it was very difficult for me to read this chapter dispassionately, because it reflected so much of my lived experience. The work that became this chapter began out of a series of conversations and shared experience they had as "nontraditional" students in academia (221). Their stated goal is to look at how women whose work in rhetoric and composition outside the expected norms—that is to say women who work outside the tenure-track, highly-published, highly-polished norms of our field—are making their way. The authors also discuss the intersections of gender, age, and career expectation (222). The focus of this work rests squarely on active participation of nontraditional academics who are making their way in the academy, rather than "passively hoping the system will change" (224). The authors collected their data from a survey (helpfully reproduced in an appendix) and by arriving at a definition of "nontraditional" (224). They found that most of the women they surveyed were aware of the risks of entering academia at an age older than the norm, but that most said they would do it again (226). Moreover, ageism is difficult to pinpoint in the academy because work outside or before entering academia is typically undervalued, but the intellectual curiosity of nontraditional women is valued (232–235). Further, the authors argue that there is a need for more study of nontraditional labor and ways of making it in the academy (238). Because the organization of the piece is extremely strong, this could serve as a model for work by readers of the *Community Literacy Journal*. But this piece also reminds us that the conversations we have with colleagues, peers, and friends can be viable starting points for research.

The collection ends strongly, just as it began strongly with "Making It as a Female Writing Program Administrator: Using Collective Action and Feminist Mentoring Practices to Transgress Gendered Boundaries," written by Angela Clark-Oates, Bre Garrett, Magdelyn Hammond Helwig, Aurora Matzke, Sherry Rankins-Robertson, and Carey Smitherman Clark. This work takes as its focus the "abysmal" failures of academic traditions to foster inclusion and diversity; these traditions have particularly failed women of color (245). The authors describe the need for an "intersectional army" to combat these traditions of exclusivity and exclusion and they specifically discuss the "necessity of intra- and interinstitutional, micro-co-mentoring to promote feminist leaders, structures, and communities of well-being" (246). After a robust literature review of specific ways higher education has failed to create diversity across its structures (246–249), "the six authors offer vignettes of experiences...that we have encountered and shared with one another during our time as WPAs" (249). These vignettes offer a varied (and frustrating) window into the world of women WPAs, but the authors all shared one common experience, "we each have experienced varying degrees of difficulty at the hands of senior females in positions of power across our campuses" (253). This common experience signals that not only are structures of inequality damaging to us all, but that there is more work to be done. In the remainder of the article, they offer several strategies for alternative leadership and for making it as female WPAs, which include co-mentoring with other WPAs, participating in workshops for WPAs, and an invitation to collaborate with the authors because WPAs know what it is like to work as a WPA, so we can offer each other support that other academics might not understand.

That invitation at the end Chapter thirteen echoes the entire collection in *Women's Ways of Making*. There is work that remains for all of us, but as this collection exemplifies, and at times exhorts us to, we can do this work together, by collaborating and mentoring and attending to the embodied ways of making in academia. I would hope to see other collections such as this because there are more ways of making it in the academy than I could have imagined.

Works Cited

Britton, Lauren. "Power, Access, Status: The Discourse of Race, Gender, and Class in the Maker Movement." *Technology and Social Change Group University of Washington, Information School*, 18 March 2015, https://tascha.uw.edu/power-access-status-the-discourse-of-race-gender-and-class-in-the-maker-movement/.

Stoller, Debbie. *Stitch 'n Bitch Crochet: The Happy Hooker*. Workman Publishing Company, 2006.

—. *Stitch 'n Bitch: The Knitter's Handbook*. Workman Publishing Company, 2004.

Writing for Love and Money: How Migration Drives Literacy Learning in Transnational Families

Kate Vieira
Oxford UP, 2019, pp. 200

KATE VIEIRA

Reviewed by Jagadish Paudel
The University of Texas at El Paso

Along with migration, digital writing has become a part of everyday reality. As people around the world have increasingly been migrating to different countries in search of a better life and more money, digital literacy is being used to strengthen love and stay in touch with family members who are physically far away. Kate Vieira's *Writing for Love and Money: How Migration Drives Literacy Learning in Transnational Families* focuses on digital literacy fostered by migration. Vieira discusses how migration results from economic inequalities in Latvia, Brazil, and the United States, how migration brought about a new kind of literacy (digital) for fulfilling emotional communication (love), and how family members learn to write and learn to keep in touch with their relatives who reside in foreign countries to earn money and seek a better life. In my own case, this seems spot-on. During two years of study here in the U.S., I saved a little money from my teaching assistantship stipend and bought two mobile phones (a Samsung for my mother and an iPhone for my wife) and a tablet (for my nephew). Last summer I went to Nepal and while there I opened a Facebook account for my mother and then taught her about using Facebook and calling via its Messenger app. Now she is able to call us (both video and audio) via Facebook Messenger and check postings for updates to know the latest news from her relatives.

Vieira carried the study she describes in the book out by collecting data from transnational families through life-history interviews and field research from 2011 to 2016. Vieira's results disprove the theory that the migration of knowledge workers to developed countries results in a "brain drain" in the homeland. Instead, Vieira argues that migration is supportive for literacy development since migration "[promotes] experiences of literacy learning in transnational families as they learn new ways of writing to reach the two life goals that globalization consistently threatens: economic solvency [money] and emotional intimacy [love]" (2). Vieira's research reveals that familial separation through migration has resulted in upward social mobility in the families studied, which leads to learning new kinds of literacies for the family members.

The book is organized into five chapters. In chapter one "What's New about Writing for Love and Money?", drawing ideas from social literacy practices, Vieira details how transnational families write and learn for love and money. Vieira describes how migration is fostering new forms of literacy, for instance, the use of remitted webcams from a sister allowing a young boy to become an expert at IT and ultimately to open his own IT business and earn money; the computer class taken by a Latvian mother to learn computer literacy in order to keep touch with her son who immigrated to Belgium; the letter written by a teenager from the United States to send to his younger sister in Mexico, teaching her some new words in English. As an international student coming from Nepal, a developing country, I was particularly fascinated by the research findings—that digital literacy has been promoted to strengthen love and keep in touch with family members and relatives. For the last few years, I have been observing many international migrants, including students and full-time job holders, sending electronic gadgets (mobile phones, laptops, tablets, etc.) and money to their families. In my case, as I mentioned in the beginning, the process described in the book is mirrored in my life, as my migration has been key to learning digital literacy for my mother and sharing love between us (me, my wife, and my three-and-a-half-year-old daughter).

In chapter two, "Writing for Love and Money on Three Continents," Vieira describes the three locations in which she conducted research: Jau in Sao Paulo, Brazil (South America); Daugavpils in Latvia (Europe); and Wisconsin in the United States (North America). At the onset of the chapter, she discusses a bit about the theory of comparing cases, that is, comparative case study research—comparing and contrasting one locale with what happened in other places and historical moments. Vieira explains multiple dimensions (across history, across scale, and across sites) of the phenomenon, which helped her "see migration-driven literacy learning across people's lifespans (transversal); among people differently positioned in relation to the forces of globalization (vertical); and across differently positioned communities in Brazil, Latvia, and the United States (horizontal)" (34). Further, Vieira discusses her research design and why she uses a lifespan approach to ethnographic research. She conducts literacy history interviews (LHIs)—a distinctive research tool that elicits memories from participants. She further conducts ethnographic fieldwork and collects data by talking with participants, taking notes on their reading and writing, interacting with them, and asking them for the opportunity to follow up with questions in formal and informal interviews. The chapter offers readers social, historical, and geographical information on how Vieira situated herself while carrying out the study. Her personal association with these communities gives her a sense of urgency and responsibility to carry out research and learn how migration-driven literacy learning operates. Overall, Vieira embraces an ethnographic approach to research design, presents a holistic view of the researched phenomenon, collects data from multiple dimensions of the phenomenon, and conducts research that spans multiple years.

In chapter three, "Learning to Log On: From Post to Internet in Brazil," Vieira discusses migration-driven digital literacy learning experiences in Brazil. From the life history interviews, Vieira obtained information about participants' experiences of using different modes of communication, for example, the participants' experience of writing letters, using phone cards, using the Internet, receiving emails, chatting, and logging on to synchronous video calls. Vieira's discussion of shifting modes of communication reminds readers, particularly those who were born before 1990, how quickly modes of communication altered from letter to video chat. Vieira expounds on the effect of technological changes in the Internet era and how labor, learning, and laptops altered educational experiences. Because of the availability of polymedia and access to the Internet, a change occurred in communication. Due to the change, for instance, mothers of migrants were afforded the opportunity to engage with their children or grandchildren who reside in foreign lands. The remittance of laptops, in particular, ensures the development of new kinds of literacies in transnational families. Vieira also describes her own example of giving laptops as a writing remittance to her brother-in-law in 2004 and to a friend in Brazil. Similarly, she discusses the materiality of writing remittances (i.e., pencils, lined paper, computers, phones) and describes how capitalist production imperatives can result in the unequal distribution of literacy technologies. Vieira presents a comparison of different transnational families' social classes with whom she worked, and her comparison showed none of the wealthier families received hardware from their family members who were in study abroad, since the families could buy the hardware themselves. This helps readers to understand unequal economic distributions and its relation to sponsoring digital gadgets for enhancing the lives of middle and lower-class families. It can be further understood that the migration of middle and lower-class families to developed countries has been a sponsor for enhancing digital literacy among their family members, and thus, helping a bit in reducing the digital divide globally. From the chapter, it is apparent how capitalism is pervasive in sponsoring literacy technologies in people's lives.

In chapter four, "Learning Languages: From Soviet Union to European Union in Latvia," Vieira documents how migration drives digital and multilingual literacy learning experiences in Latvia. Particularly, Vieira discusses three kinds of migration-driven literacy learning in Latvia: migration-driven print literacy, digital literacy, and anticipatory literacy. Among the three, the development of anticipatory literacy is pervasive in developing countries. Vieira states that anticipatory literacy learning resulted due to the fear of the eventuality of needing to migrate. She discusses how parents, in particular, were preparing their children for possible migration. Her research reveals that parents were orienting their children to learn multiple languages (e.g., English, German). Hence, their children were taking English classes, creating blogs to showcase English competency, and taking tests for going abroad—all in anticipation that they may need to migrate elsewhere. The instance that Vieira brings up here portrays the current situation of people in developing countries—they hold hope to travel to developed countries and prepare accordingly.

In chapter five, "Teaching Homeland Family: Love and Money in the United States," Vieira presents the perspective of two multigenerational migrant families in

Wisconsin in the United States with regard to migration-driven literacy learning experiences. Vieira presents migration as a fund of knowledge that is gained through lived experience, since writing remittance travels across borders and can foster a binational and bidirectional educational exchange. She shows that migrants contribute to the literacy enhancement of transnational families. Vieira finds that, despite experiencing exploitative conditions and financial hardships in the U.S., an immigrant, Carolina, from Mexico managed to be supportive to her family back in Mexico. Vieira presents the story of Carolina and Jose, Carolina's brother, to talk about writing remittances—support for writing by giving money, sending hardware (e.g., laptops), and teaching. Carolina supports her family members back home, for instance, she taught her sister English. Carolina's brother, Jose, seeks to use his law degree to empower migrants from his hometown to demand fair treatment and pay. Chapter five reminds readers of the difficult situation of immigrants—who hail from lower-class families and work in the labor force in foreign lands—to showcase how they are supporting and enhancing their family members' literacy.

In the conclusion section, "Migration-Driven Literacy Learning in Uncertain Times," Vieira explains that as globalization is increasing, writing and learning for love and money matters to all people who migrate across borders—and their family members who reside back in their respective homelands. Due to migration, literacy coursed through the lives of families that were separated across borders, and this expanded and proliferated their literacy. Seeing the phenomenon of migration in this way, Vieira argues that the brains of the people who have migrated have not been drained. Rather, migration has tied up their love, enhancing digital literacy as all family members must increasingly use digital tools to communicate.

From my observation, many Nepali immigrants come from Nepal every year to the U.S., whether through the Diversity Immigrant Visa Program (DV Program), student visas, or by taking illegal routes. Upon their arrival, no matter how much financial hardship they have, they manage to send their families some digital gadgets (laptops, tablets, watches, mobile phones, etc.) and sometimes money. The people who earn a great deal of money through their endeavors often donate to and sponsor their native country's institutions (schools, colleges, etc.), for example, either by constructing buildings or providing resources. Those people who are in academia—with limited financial resources—also contribute to their native countries in different ways, for instance, by conducting workshops virtually, giving presentations, serving as editors, and many other concrete ways. In my case, I have been serving by giving presentations in my area of expertise and working as an editor and reviewer for journals, and sharing academic resources. These life experiences demonstrate that "migration is not an educational problem to be solved, but instead as an educational resource to be supported" (Vieira 14). In other words, Vieira's book explores the idea of migration as a means to sponsoring literacy. Deborah Brandt's theory of literacy sponsorship is a pervasive thread in the sense that remittances and supporting family members, through enhancing digital literacy in one's home country, can be considered a form of literacy sponsorship. Across the world, migration is accelerating daily as people search for jobs, education, and a better life. Though data were collected in three places, Vieira's book represents real scenarios that have become common across the world. This book shows how literacy develops outside the classroom and provides some research avenues that could guide future scholars in the same vein. Vieira provides sufficient information to understand the research sites, the participants, and other needed information to comprehend and apply the author's research methods. I found her research to be based on strong, solid ethnographic methods.

However, as a reader, I also noticed some weaknesses in the book. For example, Vieira presented the research method she uses in the Appendix section. As a reader, I think it would be helpful to incorporate the research methods within each chapter so that readers can understand the methods alongside her comparative case studies. Additionally, Vieira focuses on the positive side of migration-driven literacy; however, her book does not delve into the often heart-wrenching situation of many immigrant people's parents in their home countries, not having anyone to take care of them in their old age. Another vital aspect is that as young literate people leave their home countries in search of better jobs and opportunities, immigrants are losing their indigenous literacy and knowledge. Nonetheless, given that Vieira discusses the relationship between migration and literacy development, this book is essential reading for graduate students, researchers, and teachers who are interested in migration-driven digital literacy. This book is even more useful for community literacy researchers, as it describes how a researcher situates herself to carry out ethnographic research in different communities and the broader theoretical implications of that research.

PARLOR PRESS
EQUIPMENT FOR LIVING

Now with Parlor Press!

Studies in Rhetorics and Feminism
    Series Editors: Cheryl Glenn and Shirley Wilson Logan

Emerging Conversations in the Global Humanities
    Series Editor: Victor E. Taylor

The X-Series
    Series Editor: Jordan Frith

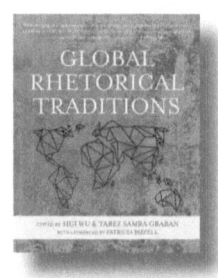

New Releases

Reimagining the Humanities, edited by Barry Mauer and Anastasia Salter

Global Rhetorical Traditions, edited by Hui Wu and Tarez Samra Graban

Rhetorical Listening in Action: A Concept-Tacticc Approach by Krista Ratcliffe and Kyle Jensen

A Rhetoric of Becoming: USAmerican Women in Qatar by Nancy Small

MLA Mina Shaughnessy Prize and CCCC Best Book Award 2021!

Creole Composition: Academic Writing and Rhetoric in the Anglophone Caribbean, edited by Vivette Milson-Whyte, Raymond Oenbring, and Brianne Jaquette

Check Out Our New Website!

Discounts, blog, open access titles, instant downloads, and more.

www.parlorpress.com

Community Literacy Journal Discount: Use CLJ20 at checkout to receive a 20% discount on all titles not on sale through March 15, 2023.

www.ingramcontent.com/pod-product-compliance
Lightning Source LLC
Chambersburg PA
CBHW020216170426
43199CB00029B/343